# DETERRENTS

### AND

# REINFORCEMENT

*Stanford Studies in Psychology, II*

EDITORS
Robert R. Sears
Leon Festinger
Douglas H. Lawrence

# DETERRENTS

and

# REINFORCEMENT

*The Psychology of Insufficient Reward*

Douglas H. Lawrence

*and*

Leon Festinger

STANFORD UNIVERSITY PRESS

STANFORD, CALIFORNIA

1962

Stanford University Press
Stanford, California

© 1962 by the Board of Trustees of the
Leland Stanford Junior University

*Library of Congress Catalog Card Number: 62-8664*

Printed in the United States of America

# Preface

About four years ago it occurred to us that the theory of dissonance, which seems to explain some unusual human behavior quite well, might be relevant to some bothersome data concerning extinction in animals. Our enthusiasm for the idea was not, at the time, completely unrestrained. On the one hand, the idea seemed to have good possibilities of explaining some of the theoretical problems connected with the consequences of partial reward. On the other hand, it seemed somewhat unusual to apply a theory developed on the basis of human behavior to explain rat behavior. And, in addition, could we seriously assume that rats reacted to dissonance in the way that human beings do?

Nevertheless, we proceeded to investigate the idea. We searched the existing literature and were encouraged. We started to do some preliminary, exploratory experiments of our own and were further encouraged. The present book reports the results of our four years of research. In the course of these four years our ideas became considerably clarified, suggesting new extensions of the theory, and new experiments. We performed a total of sixteen experiments which are reported in this book.

It would be unfortunate to give the impression that this book is solely the product of the two authors. A number of people were active collaborators in the experimentation. A majority of the experiments we report were done in collaboration with John M. Theios and Edward Uyeno. Theios was also responsible for the idea of the "partially placed" condition in Experiment 15.

There were many others who also helped in various aspects of the experimental work. We should like to express our thanks to Elaine Hatfield, William Lawton, Peter Polson, James Schoonard, Bernard Sjoberg, Herbert Smith, Laurence Stettner, and Neil Sullivan. We also wish to thank Gordon H. Bower, William K. Estes, Frank J. Restle, and Robert R. Sears for reading the manuscript of this book and offering many constructive and helpful suggestions.

We should also like to express our appreciation to the National Institutes of Health (Grant M-1689 to Douglas H. Lawrence) and to the Ford Foundation (a grant to Leon Festinger) for liberally supporting our work.

DOUGLAS H. LAWRENCE
LEON FESTINGER

PALO ALTO, CALIFORNIA
July 4, 1961

# Contents

# Contents

# DETERRENTS

## AND

# REINFORCEMENT

# 1

# An Impasse for Learning Theory

A major function of theory in any science is the integration and explanation of diverse empirical relationships. In its early stages a scientific theory may deal with a few variables in an attempt to account for data in a delimited area. When a theory becomes highly developed it usually encompasses a large number of variables and, from the hypothesized interrelationships among these variables, is able to integrate and explain a large number of observed phenomena. Needless to say, the growth of a theory from its beginning stages to a point where it may be termed highly developed is beset with many difficulties. The course of development is never smooth.

No sooner does a theory establish itself as being able to explain a given body of data than there begins to appear evidence that is apparently inconsistent with it. Sometimes this new evidence points to a new variable that must be incorporated into the theory; sometimes the new evidence leads to a minor modification of the assumptions underlying the theory; and sometimes there is no clear way to change or enlarge the theory so as to take into account the new and contradictory evidence. When the latter is the case, the theory usually continues to be developed along its own lines, contradictory evidence simply being ignored. But this new evidence also continues to accumulate until it is no longer merely "new" but is an established and considerable body of knowledge. Then an impasse is reached. Progress becomes very difficult until some major modification or extension of the theory is invented. In the field of psychology there are few theories that have been developed to a point where such an impasse is even possible. In the field of learning, however, theory has been developed this far. And, unfortunately, just such an impasse has been reached.

It is the purpose of this chapter to point out the nature and locus of this impasse. We shall review first some of the major assumptions underlying learning theory. We shall then show that these assumptions stand in apparent opposition to some well-established experimental results.

It will be the purpose of the remainder of this volume to suggest a major theoretical extension that reconciles these data and assumptions. In addition, we shall present a considerable amount of new data that provides added support for the theoretical extension we are offering.

## The Focus of Learning Theory

It is difficult to summarize "learning theory" in general since there is still no single uniformly accepted theoretical statement. There is, however, a core of theory that stems from the work of Hull (1943). Although there are exceptions among learning theorists, these core assumptions are widely accepted, and it is this core to which we shall address ourselves.

Learning theory is, of course, concerned basically with the explanation of how the behavior of an organism is progressively modified as the result of experiential factors. Such modification of behavior obviously involves increasing frequency of some actions and decreasing frequency of other actions in any given situation. In giving a theoretical account of such changes, it proved useful very early in the development of learning theory to think in terms of a concept that may be called "response strength," representing the magnitude of the tendency for a given response to be evoked in a given situation. It, of course, became necessary to specify how response strength can be measured. Three measures of response strength have been commonly used. All of them are plausible and have been proved valid by data.

1. *Relative frequency of response.*—It has been plausibly argued that the stronger a response tendency is, the more likely is the response to be elicited by the stimulus with which it is

associated. In the early stages of establishing an association between a stimulus and a response this does indeed seem to be a good measure. For example, in discrimination-learning problems, maze-learning situations, or situations where the organism has to learn to make one of a number of possible instrumental responses, the relative frequency with which the response occurs upon presentation of the stimulus is an excellent indicator of the course of learning. The data show that as the number of stimulus-response sequences that have been rewarded increases, there is an increase in the likelihood that the "correct" response will be elicited upon a subsequent presentation of the stimulus. This measure of response strength, however, seems to be a sensitive measure only rather early in the learning process.

2. *Latency of response.*—It has been plausibly argued that the stronger the response strength the less time will elapse between presentation of the stimulus and the elicitation of the response. This measure has proved to be rather generally useful and also quite sensitive. As the number of rewarded stimulus-response sequences increases, the latency of the response becomes shorter and shorter until it reaches some stable value. At the beginning stages of learning there are usually very marked changes in latency, and, in addition, this measure continues to show progressive changes toward shorter and shorter times, even after relative frequency of response has reached 100 per cent.

3. *Resistance to extinction.*—A third generally accepted measure of response strength is resistance to extinction. Let us imagine that a given stimulus-response sequence has been rewarded a large number of times and, consequently, the response strength is relatively strong. If we continued to elicit the response by presenting the stimulus, but never again provided any reward in the situation, we would expect the animal to persist in its behavior until the response strength had weakened sufficiently. Starting with a response of considerable strength, it might take many trials before the animal stopped responding. On the other hand, if the response strength had been quite weak at the beginning of the series of unrewarded elicitations of the response, we would expect extinction to occur much more rapidly. Thus, the resistance that the animal shows to extinction

can be taken as a measure of the response strength at the beginning of the series of unrewarded experiences.

Thus, we have three measures of response strength.* Although all of these measures are operationally independent,
theoretically they are all measures of the same thing and should,
of course, be interrelated in predictable ways. As response
strength increases because of the occurrence of stimulus-response sequences followed by reward, the relative frequency
of response should increase, latency of response should simultaneously decrease, and subsequent tests should show that the
response is more resistant to extinction. It is, of course, possible
to uncorrelate these three measures, as shown by the work of
Logan (1960) and others, and clearly each of these is more
appropriate to some experimental arrangements than to others.
Nonetheless, these relationships do tend to be characteristic of
most learning situations.

With the use of this concept of response strength, the basic
task for the field of learning became the specification of those
variables that strengthen and those that weaken it. The problem for learning theory was to integrate these variables into a
useful explanatory system. Over the years a number of fairly
extensive theories have been developed that effectively deal
with many of these variables. These theories differ in a variety
of aspects, but they do have many assumptions in common.
This is not surprising since they all try to account for the same
set of experimental results. These assumptions, held in common
by most theorists, are, however, precisely the ones that seem to
be clearly contradicted by a variety of empirical findings. In
reviewing these assumptions, we shall be very brief, ignoring
many of the more subtle points of controversy and interpretation that have centered around them.

1. *The function of reward.*—It has been known for a long
time that if an organism is motivated, perhaps by hunger, and
some response that it makes is followed by an appropriate re-

---

* A fourth measure of "response strength," namely, amplitude of response,
has also been employed frequently. Since this particular measure is not relevant
to the kinds of experimental situations with which we shall deal, we shall not
discuss it further.

ward, such as food, the likelihood that the organism will perform this action again is increased. Thus, most theories of learning propose that if, in a given situation, a response is followed
by reward, the response strength increases. It is also well known
that if a response in a situation is not followed by a reward appropriate to the motivation of the organism, the likelihood that
the organism will again perform that action is diminished.
Learning theory has therefore adopted a proposition to deal
appropriately with this phenomenon. In short, in order to account for known data concerning rewards in a learning situation, learning theory proposes that if a response is followed by
a reward, response strength is increased; if not followed by a
reward, response strength is decreased. This basic proposition
has been very useful in helping to explain a good deal of data.

2. *Delay of reward.*—It has been observed many times that
if a reward follows a given response almost immediately, learning is very rapid. On the other hand, if there is a temporal delay between the response and the reward, learning proceeds
more slowly. In experiments on discrimination learning in rats,
for example, a delay of even a few seconds between the response
and the reward produces a considerable decrement in the rate
at which the response is learned. In order to account for these
data, learning theories generally agree on what may be called a
"gradient of reward effect." The theoretical proposition is that
a given reward produces the greatest increment of response
strength if the reward immediately follows the response. The
longer the time that elapses between the performance of the
response and the occurrence of the reward, the smaller is the
ensuing increment in response strength. This theoretical statement has been tested extensively, and we may feel confident
that it is valid.

3. *Effort expenditure.*—There is one more variable that we
should like to mention at this point. Although it is not nearly
so central to learning theory as the two variables we have
already discussed, nevertheless it is important and well documented. Experimental studies have shown rather consistently
that the more effort a response demands, the less willing is the
animal to make the response. Learning tends to proceed more

slowly the greater the effort involved in the response. Some theories of learning have proposed that effort increases response inhibition. Other theories have been inclined to regard effort as a negative incentive. But, in one form or another, most learning theories include the proposition that increased effort weakens the response strength.

These three variables—reward, delay of reward, and effortfulness of response—are, of course, only a small part of what is dealt with by learning theory. We have mentioned these three because they are the ones that are so integrally involved in the theoretical difficulties with which we are concerned.

## A Major Difficulty for Learning Theory

Recently, there has accumulated a considerable body of experimental evidence suggesting that these common assumptions underlying learning theory fail to give an adequate description of changes in response strength. In fact, there is the suggestion that under some circumstances the variables of reward, temporal delay, and effort may have just the opposite effects from those predicted by the assumptions we have outlined. The problem, and its seriousness, can best be illustrated by describing three lines of experimental work.

1. *The effects of partial reward.*—Partial reward refers to a training procedure in which only a proportion of the stimulus-response sequences are rewarded: the occurrences of rewarded and unrewarded trials are randomly determined so that an animal cannot anticipate the outcome on any given trial. For instance, a hungry rat may be trained to run a maze in order to find food in the goal box. If this training is done by means of a 50 per cent reward schedule, there will be food in the goal box on only half the trials. On the other half of the trials, the box will be empty. The important theoretical issue centers about the question of the response strength at the end of training when a partial reward schedule has been used in contrast to a 100 per cent reward schedule, that is, one on which the animal is rewarded on every trial.

The theoretical issue was forced on the attention of learning theorists by the early studies of Humphreys (1939) and others (cf. Jenkins and Stanley, 1950, and Lewis, 1960). It became apparent that there was a direct conflict between theory and data. Learning theory predicted that performance should be of maximum strength with a 100 per cent reward schedule, in which every trial was rewarded, and of less strength after a partial reward schedule in which rewarded and unrewarded trials are intermixed. The experimental data, on the other hand, indicated that just the converse was true. A partial reward schedule established a stronger performance than did continuous reward when response strength was measured by resistance to extinction. These data indicated that there was something wrong with those theoretical assumptions that say response strength increases as the number of reward experiences increases, and decreases with the accumulation of non-reward experiences.

To make the issue somewhat more concrete, let us review a recent study done by Weinstock (1954). He trained four groups of hungry rats to run an alleyway for food. The percentage of trials on which each group was rewarded was, respectively, 100 per cent, 80 per cent, 50 per cent, and 30 per cent. Only one trial a day was given until each animal had had 75 trials. All groups were then run for an additional 20 trials without reward. On each trial of training and extinction a speed score was recorded.

Under these training conditions, it is clear what the assumptions underlying learning theory should predict about the strength of performance at the end of 75 trials. The 100 per cent reward group has had 75 rewarded trials, and if performance strength is a cumulative function of reward, this group should show the strongest tendency to run and to persist in this response. On the other hand, the 30 per cent reward group has had only about 23 rewarded trials, far fewer than the 100 per cent reward group, in which to build up performance strength. Furthermore, it has had 52 unrewarded trials, each of which should have subtracted from the response strength. Consequently, at the end of training it should show relatively poor performance as measured both by the latency of the response and by resistance to extinction.

The main results of this study only partially support this theoretical expectation. At the end of training the speed scores indicated that the 100 per cent reward group was, indeed, fastest. Then came the 80 per cent, 50 per cent, and 30 per cent reward groups, in order. Thus, in terms of this latency or speed measure there is good support for the theoretical prediction that the more frequently rewarded group should have the stronger tendency to run. However, if we look at a measure of resistance to extinction we get just the opposite ordering of the groups. Using an arbitrary criterion of extinction (a speed score of 0.2), this criterion is reached on the fourth trial by the 100 per cent group, on the twelfth trial by the 80 per cent group, on the eighteenth trial by the 50 per cent group, and not at all during the twenty trials by the 30 per cent reward group. Thus, there are clear and marked differences among the groups in their tendency to persist in this behavior. The group rewarded most *infrequently* was the *most* resistant to extinction. In theoretical terms, it means that the partially rewarded groups had greater response strength than did the 100 per cent reward group. These results are very difficult to reconcile with the theories of learning.

There is nothing artifactual about the Weinstock experiment. The same results occur over and over again in the literature. In most of these studies, we find that at the end of training the 100 per cent reward group runs faster than the partially rewarded group, just as in Weinstock's experiment. And in practically all studies, the partially rewarded group is more resistant to extinction than is the 100 per cent reward group.

2. *The effect of delay of reward.*—A similar and equally difficult problem confronts us in a number of recent studies on delay of reward. This latter term refers to a training procedure in which an interval of time is interposed between the performance of the response and the presentation of the reward. For example, a hungry animal may be trained to run to a goal box where it is restrained for twenty to thirty seconds before being given food. As we have indicated previously, learning theory assumes that the longer this delay of reward, the smaller is the increment of response strength. Rewards are most effective

when they are immediate. It has been known for a long time that delay of reward during training slows the rate of learning and produces relatively long latencies in the performance of the response. It is precisely these findings that give strong support to some of the assumptions of learning theory.

Recently, however, there have been investigations of the effect of these delays on resistance to extinction. When this measure of response strength is used, the experimental results are again in direct opposition to our theoretical expectations. A group of animals trained with delay intervals between the response and the reward shows more persistence during extinction than does a comparable group that has had immediate reward on each training trial. This finding has been replicated sufficiently often by now that we can have complete faith in it. But if this is true, it contradicts learning theory. It indicates that a delay in reward has increased, not decreased, the strength of the tendency to perform the response.

The problem involved can best be underlined by describing an experiment on delay of reward. Wike and McNamara (1957) did a study to determine the effect on resistance to extinction of differing percentages of trials on which delay of reward was present. They trained three groups of hungry animals on a runway. One group was delayed for thirty seconds on 25 per cent of the trials before entering the goal box and finding food. On the remaining trials, no delay at all was involved. These delay and no-delay trials occurred in an unpredictable order. The second group was delayed for thirty seconds on 50 per cent of its trials, and the third group on 75 per cent of its trials.

According to learning theory, we should expect the third group, which experienced the greatest number of delays, to have the weakest response strength and the first group, which experienced the fewest delay trials, to have the strongest. Again we find that measures of latency of response during training support the learning theory prediction. At the end of 28 training trials, the running times were fastest for the group with the least percentage of delay and slowest for the group with the greatest percentage of delay. However, once more we find a contradiction between theory and performance during extinction. Resistance to extinction is least for those with the fewest delay trials (25 per cent delay group) and greatest for those with the most delay trials (75 per cent delay group). Thus, this study clearly indicates that the more frequently an animal has experienced delay of reward the greater is its persistence during extinction. This outcome is very difficult to reconcile with the assumptions that learning theory makes about the effects of the gradient of reward on response strength.

It should be emphasized that this type of result has been obtained so frequently that it can be accepted as a generalization. The partial delay aspect of the above experiment is not a crucial feature. The same result obtains even when one group is delayed on each training trial and the other group is never delayed (Fehrer, 1956). Thus, granting that resistance to extinction is a valid index of response strength, we are confronted by the dilemma that delay of reward strengthens performance when on theoretical grounds we have every right to expect that it would weaken it.

3. *The effect of effort.*—A third area of conflict between theory and empirical findings concerns the effect of effort on response strength. Here it must be granted that the experimental evidence is scanty. Nonetheless, there are sufficient data to suggest that future findings will be a source of embarrassment to learning theory.

We have indicated that effort is conceptualized in learning theory as a negative incentive or else as a variable that builds up an inhibitory state opposing the response being learned. In either instance we should expect that the more effort required of the animal in order to obtain a given reward, the weaker would be its response strength. And data show that effortful responses are usually learned more slowly and show longer latencies than non-effortful ones. The source of conflict between learning theory and data here again only becomes apparent when we look at the effect of effort on persistence during extinction.

One of the most clear-cut studies on the effect of effort is reported by Aiken (1957). He used an apparatus where the animal had to press against a panel in order to obtain a pellet of food. The pressure, and thus the effort, required to activate the panel could be varied. For one group of animals, 32 grams of pressure were required during training whereas for the other group only 5 grams were required. After training, the animals were extinguished to a criterion of two consecutive failures to respond within thirty seconds. During the extinction trials half of each training group was required to exert 5 grams of pressure and the other half, 32 grams of pressure.

The 5-gram and the 32-gram training groups differ, as one would expect, in how quickly they learn. The group exerting greater effort learns more slowly. During extinction, however, there are clear differences in persistence that are contrary to theoretical expectation. The data from this experiment are shown in Table 1.1.

TABLE 1.1

AVERAGE NUMBER OF TRIALS TO EXTINCTION
(*From Aiken, 1957*)

| Effort During Extinction | Effort During Acquisition | |
| --- | --- | --- |
| | 5 grams | 32 grams |
| 5 grams | 45.5 | 56.5 |
| 32 grams | 35.6 | 46.8 |

Let us look first at the figures in the upper left and lower right quadrants. It is clear from the data that when animals are extinguished under the same effort condition on which they were trained, there is no difference in resistance to extinction. This is true even though for one group 32 grams of effort is involved and for the other only 5 grams. This is in itself somewhat surprising. If effort is a negative incentive, then a group trained and extinguished on 32 grams should certainly have less response strength than one trained and extinguished on 5 grams. This same type of result has been found by Weiss (1961), Maatsch, Adelman, and Denny (1954), and others.

Of even more importance, however, is the comparison between columns in the table. Within either row, we can compare two groups that were extinguished under exactly the same effort condition; they differ only with respect to the effort they had expended during training. In each of the two comparisons, the group that expended the most effort *during training* takes more trials to reach the criterion of extinction. If this result proves to be valid, it is disconcerting from the viewpoint of the assumptions of learning theory. The more effort the animal is required to expend during training, the less should be the strength of its response. Why, then, does it persist longer during extinction?

This brief survey is sufficient to indicate that there is a considerable body of data that represents a persistent irritant to the learning theorist. It is clear that partial reward, delay of reward, and effort are variables that increase resistance to extinction when theoretically they should decrease it.

We should like to emphasize the fundamental quality of this conflict between fact and theory. First of all, it is not as though these findings were concerned with complex phenomena relatively remote from the main areas of learning theory. If they were, we could always console ourselves with the thought that they would eventually fall into place once our theories were developed sufficiently to deal with them. Unfortunately, however, these results concern phenomena that are directly within the province of our present theories. And these theories, as they are presently formulated, make clear-cut predictions as to what should occur. The conflict between fact and prediction cannot be ignored.

Second, and probably more important, the strategy for handling this contradiction is not clear. It is simple enough to say that when a well-established fact contradicts a theoretical prediction, the assumptions of the theory should be changed. But in the present instance this procedure might well result in a very great loss for relatively little gain. The present assumptions of learning theory do account in an adequate manner for a wide range of behavior. Even more significantly, they do account adequately for some aspects of the data from partial reward, delay of reward, and effort studies. For instance, they do predict the slower learning and the longer latencies that normally are observed when these variables are introduced into the training procedure. What they fail primarily to predict is one aspect of these studies, namely, the effect of these variables on resistance to extinction. Consequently, it is not at all clear that we can make a simple change in assumptions to account for the latter effects without giving up the present predictive power for the other aspects of the behavior.

At first glance it would appear that we might circumvent the apparent contradiction by contending that resistance to extinction is a poor measure of response strength. This approach is totally unacceptable, however, because it cuts the theory loose from just those aspects of behavior that we wish to predict. No one desires this sort of solution. Furthermore, such an approach indirectly would admit that there are unknown variables, other than rewards, that can build up resistance to extinction. These other variables would have to be seen as even more potent than rewards because no accumulation of rewarded experiences ever makes a 100 per cent reward group as resistant to extinction as a partially rewarded one.

## Attempted Explanations

The contradiction between learning theory and data has stimulated many people to try to find some explanation. These explanations have centered, almost exclusively, on the data concerning partial reward. The reason for this exclusive focus is historically simple. The partial reward effect was the first one to be noted, whereas the data concerning the effect of delay of reward are relatively recent. The role that effort has in increasing resistance to extinction has been largely overlooked in spite of the data in the literature.

The task for those who have attempted to explain these apparent contradictions has not been an easy one. The explanations that have been offered represented great theoretical ingenuity and were, on the whole, adequate to explain what was known at the time. Like all good explanations, they stimulated further research. Unfortunately, this further research tended to make them less tenable. Nonetheless, it is because of these explanations that there is now sufficient data to permit new explanations. We shall review the past critically for the purpose of providing a background for the explanation we wish to offer.

Attempts to explain the partial reward effect have been so numerous that it is not feasible to review all of them. We shall review, and attempt to evaluate, those that have seemed most plausible and have gained at least temporary acceptance. We shall concentrate on those that have led to current formulations and, of course, on those that are still current.

*The Humphreys Hypothesis.*—One of the earliest explanations of the partial reward effect was suggested by Humphreys (1939). In an experiment using human eye-blink conditioning, Humphreys demonstrated clearly that resistance to extinction was greater after a sequence in which, on some occasions, the conditioned stimulus was not followed by a puff of air to the eye than after a sequence in which the puff always followed the conditioned stimulus. To account for this he offered an explanation that has provided the basis for much of the subsequent theorizing about the effects of partial reward.

According to Humphreys, the subject continues to respond until he has had sufficient experience with the conditions during extinction to convince himself that the reinforcing event no longer occurs in this situation. This explanation can account for the difference in resistance to extinction between a 100 per cent rewarded group and a partially rewarded one. A given reward is present on every training trial for the 100 per cent group, and then it is suddenly removed when extinction trials begin. This sharp and sudden change of stimulus conditions permits these subjects to realize quickly that there has been a change. For the partially rewarded subjects, however, there is less change in the stimulus conditions between the training trials and the extinction trials. During the training trials the subjects frequently experience omission of reward, and therefore extinction trials do not represent a totally new situation for these individuals. This overlap in stimulus conditions makes it difficult for them to discriminate between the end of training and the beginning of extinction. This greater difficulty of discrimination reveals itself as a slower rate of extinction.

There are really two aspects to this explanation of extinction effects that Humphreys has offered. Although they are similar in nature, it is advantageous to discuss them separately. One of these aspects we should like to call an "amount of information explanation." The other has been called a "discrimination explanation." The former says that extinction occurs only when the subject has had sufficient experience to expect consistent absence of reward. Subjects trained on a partial reward schedule have come to expect a certain number of unrewarded trials

mixed in with rewarded ones; consequently, when extinction
starts, it takes them longer to realize that reward is totally absent
than it takes subjects that have been always rewarded. If subjects are trained with a very low ratio of rewarded to unrewarded trials, extinction may take very long indeed.

This explanation, although somewhat vague, and certainly
not well integrated with conventional learning theory, does explain the major data on the partial reward effect. It does not,
of course, explain the increased resistance to extinction following delay of reward, nor does it explain the fact that increased
effort increases resistance to extinction. But these latter facts
were not known at the time when Humphreys offered his explanation. So far as data relating to the effects of partial reward
are concerned, this "information" hypothesis has never been in-
validated. Its lack of general acceptance among learning theorists may be due to a number of things. First of all, it is difficult
to integrate this idea into learning theory in any precise manner.
Second, there is undoubtedly some suspicion that the magnitude
of the effects obtained in experiments is not fully consistent with
this explanation. We shall leave it at this for now, although
later in this book we shall present new data on the basis of which
we may discard this "information explanation."

The second aspect of the explanation offered by Humphreys
has been much more widely accepted. This "discrimination explanation" focuses on the fact that there are more elements in
the situation that are common to both extinction and acquisition
for partially rewarded than for continuously rewarded subjects.
This is true whether one is dealing with eye-blink conditioning
or with a hungry animal running an alley. The common element
for the partially rewarded animal is the presence of non-rewarded trials both during training and during extinction, an
overlap that is not experienced by the continuously rewarded
one. It has long been known that an animal finds it more difficult
to establish a discrimination between two stimulus situations
that differ in only a few aspects than between two that differ
in many. Consequently, if the partially rewarded animal learns
to respond on unrewarded trials during training, it is not at all
surprising that it transfers this responding to the extinction situ-

ation to a far greater extent than does the continuously rewarded one that has never learned to respond on such trials. This "discrimination hypothesis" has been taken over in one form or another by many other theorists (Bitterman *et al.*, 1953; Mowrer, 1960).

If one examines this explanation closely, however, it turns out that it does not really relate the partial reward effect to an organized set of theoretical concepts. Actually, it is mainly an extension of an empirical generalization. We have observed in a variety of conventional discrimination experiments that the greater the similarity of the stimuli in two situations the harder it is for an animal to establish differential responses to those situations. We then observe that there is at least one sense in which the training and extinction conditions for the partially rewarded animal are more similar than they are for the continuously rewarded animal. From this we infer that the partially rewarded animal will have more difficulty in establishing differential behaviors, those of responding and not responding, in the two conditions.

There is nothing wrong in the use of such empirical generalizations. Often they are the only basis for prediction that we have. The great difficulty is that there are always gross exceptions to the rule which we tend to gloss over. An example with respect to the present generalization arises in the case of delay of reward. Wike and McNamara (1957) did a study which differed in design from the conventional one involving delay of reward. Their apparatus consisted of a runway leading into a delay compartment, which in turn exited into a goal box. The control animals ran directly through the delay compartment and immediately found food in the goal box. The experimental animals were trapped for a few seconds in the delay compartment, and then released to find food immediately in the goal box. During extinction both groups were permitted to run directly through the delay compartment into the goal box, but of course there was no longer any food.

If we ask what the similarities are between training and extinction conditions, it is clear that the two conditions are more similar for the control than for the delay group. The control group always ran directly through the delay compartment in both training and extinction conditions. The delay group, on the other hand, had been retained there during training, but *not* in extinction. Clearly, this switch from delay to no delay is an abrupt change in conditions for the latter. So, in terms of our empirical generalization, we have every right to expect that the delay animals will extinguish more rapidly than the control ones. But this is not what happens; instead, just the converse is true.

Strong believers in the "discrimination hypothesis" may not appreciate this exception to their generalization, even though in terms of "obvious" similarities the argument is impeccable. They will point to other possible similarities, such as the fact that the delay animals have experienced delay without food at least some place in the apparatus during training, whereas the control animals have not. This experience of not obtaining food, it may be argued, is the characteristic common to the training and extinction situations for the delay animals that is important in increasing resistance to extinction.

This counterargument, however, reveals the weakness of an empirical generalization as compared with a true theoretical explanation. There are always a multitude of similarities and differences between training and extinction conditions for both experimental and control animals. Consequently, depending upon which ones are picked and how they are weighted, a variety of predictions about extinction can be made. It is only when an empirical generalization of this sort can be related to an organized set of theoretical concepts that one has a criterion by means of which such a selection can be made. There have been many serious attempts to provide the needed theoretical basis for the discrimination hypothesis. We shall proceed to examine some of them.

*The Sheffield Hypothesis.*—One of the most ingenious and coherent theoretical bases for the discrimination hypothesis was proposed by Sheffield (1949). Her line of reasoning was cogent and plausible. It seems reasonable to postulate that reward and non-reward produce distinctive reactions in the animal, which in turn produce distinctive internal stimuli. The act of eating undoubtedly produces characteristic kinesthetic stimuli. The reaction to non-reward undoubtedly produces a very different but equally characteristic set of stimuli. It is also quite reasonable to assume that these characteristic internal stimuli, the aftereffects of rewarded or unrewarded trials, persist for a period of time.

With these assumptions in mind, Sheffield gave the following theoretical analysis of the training experiences of animals rewarded 100 per cent of the time and of partially rewarded animals. If animals are rewarded on every trial, they always have those stimulus aftereffects that are characteristic of eating. If these aftereffects persist until the following trial, they form part of the stimulus complex that is present when the animal again runs in the apparatus and is again rewarded. Consequently, the stimulus aftereffects of eating become associated with the running response. Partially rewarded animals, on the other hand, sometimes have stimulus aftereffects characteristic of reward and sometimes have those that are characteristic of non-reward. In so far as these persist from one trial to the following trial, each is sometimes present when the animal again runs and is rewarded. Consequently, both types of stimulus aftereffects become associated with the running response. Thus, in contrast to the continuously rewarded animal, the partially rewarded one has established two associations—namely, running in the presence of reward aftereffects and running in the presence of non-reward aftereffects.

During extinction all animals experience only the stimulus aftereffects characteristic of non-reward. These have never been associated with running for the continuously rewarded animals. Thus, in terms of the concept of stimulus generalization, there should be a decrement in the strength of the running response for these animals, and they should extinguish rapidly. On the other hand, the aftereffects of non-reward *have* been associated with running during the training of the partially rewarded animals. There is, then, little stimulus generalization decrement when extinction trials begin, and they should extinguish more slowly. Thus, a coherent theoretical account of partial reward effects was given by postulating that rewards and non-rewards produce stimulus events that persist until the start of the next trial.

The crucial assumption here concerns the persistence of these aftereffects. For both theoretical and empirical reasons, theorists have agreed that these stimulus traces are short lived, that is, they disappear within minutes or even seconds. Incorporating this knowledge concerning the durability of stimulus traces into the theoretical explanation leads to the conclusion that partial reward effects should be observed only under massed training and massed extinction conditions and should not be found when the trials are widely spaced. If spaced trials are used during training, animals that are always rewarded and animals that are partially rewarded would not have any differential stimulus traces to be associated with the running response because the stimulus aftereffects of the preceding trial would have disappeared. Thus, with widely spaced trials the partial reward effect should disappear or perhaps even be reversed.

Realizing that this derivation concerning the effects of spaced and massed trials was crucial for the explanation, Sheffield conducted an experiment to test its validity. She found that when animals were trained under conditions of massed trials (an intertrial interval of about fifteen seconds) the usual difference between partially rewarded and 100 per cent rewarded animals appeared. If, however, the animals were trained using spaced trials (an intertrial interval of fifteen to twenty minutes) there was no significant difference between the two groups in resistance to extinction.

These data, of course, gave strong support to the Sheffield explanation. If these results could be replicated, and if the Sheffield explanation could be accepted as correct, there would no longer be any contradiction at all between learning theory and the data concerning extinction after partial reward. There were, consequently, a number of attempts to repeat the Sheffield experiment. Unfortunately, the results she obtained did not stand up. We shall review some of these studies in order to give a fair picture of the evidence that has accumulated.

Two experiments directly attempted to replicate the Sheffield finding. Lewis (1956) did one of these studies using an apparatus and procedure almost identical to that used by Sheffield. The major difference between the Sheffield and the Lewis experiments was the time intervals between trials. Both experiments used a fifteen-second intertrial interval for massed training, but whereas Sheffield used a fifteen-minute interval for the spaced trials, Lewis used only a two-minute interval. Lewis found that the intertrial interval made no difference. The partially rewarded animals extinguished more slowly than those that were rewarded on every trial, regardless of the intertrial interval.

Wilson, Weiss, and Amsel (1955) replicated the Sheffield experiment using no procedural variations whatsoever. They used the same kind of apparatus, the same procedure, and the same time intervals that Sheffield had used. They also found that the intertrial interval, that is, whether the training trials were massed or spaced, made no difference at all. Regardless of the intertrial interval, the partially rewarded animals showed themselves to be more resistant to extinction than those that had been rewarded 100 per cent of the time during training. These failures to replicate the Sheffield result suggest that her finding may have been due to sampling error.

The final blow to the Sheffield hypothesis as an adequate explanation of partial reward effects was given by the Weinstock experiment to which we have previously referred. When he demonstrated that clear-cut effects of partial reward on extinction were obtained even though training trials were spaced twenty-four hours apart, it no longer was possible to believe in a hypothesis that made the intertrial interval the crucial variable.

We have reviewed only a few of the many studies that have been done in the last ten years. An examination of all the research leads Lewis to say: "The conclusion seems to be rather firm that the PRE [partial reward effect] obtains whatever the spacing of the acquisition trials." (Lewis, 1960, p. 10.) One must conclude that the Sheffield interpretation must be discarded as an explanation for the effects of partial reward.

*"Competing Response" Hypotheses.*—Several theorists have offered explanations of the partial reward effect that circumvent the need for having stimulus traces persist between trials. Some of these theories are based on the idea that unrewarded trials produce competing responses which are either adapted out or

conditioned to running on subsequent rewarded trials. Weinstock (1954) has emphasized the adaptation to non-reward. Estes (1959) has emphasized the other possibility. We shall base our discussion here mainly on the statement by Estes, which represents a more complete theoretical account. Estes says:

According to the present theory, the mechanism for extinction of an instrumental response is conceived as follows. The function of non-reinforcement is to establish a stimulating situation in which competing responses have high probabilities. When the competing responses are evoked in the presence of stimulus elements which are connected to the formerly reinforced response, conditioning occurs in accordance with the contiguity principle, and the competing responses gain connections at the expense of the formerly reinforced one. During a series of reinforced trials, some one response, e.g., approaching a food tray, becomes well conditioned to the reinforcing situation, e.g., the goal box of a maze. Then when reinforcement is first omitted, cues from the changed situation and cues arising from the disrupted response sequence evoke competing responses with high probability. Consequently, extinction tends to be rapid following a series of continuously reinforced trials. Under a partial reinforcement schedule, the situation is somewhat different. Competing responses which become conditioned following a non-reinforcement early in the series will tend to occur on later reinforced trials; therefore, response-produced stimuli associated with them will become conditioned cues for the reinforced response and will tend to maintain the latter during a subsequent extinction series. (P. 437.)

In brief, the idea is that an unrewarded trial tends to evoke responses in the animal that compete with the response of running to the goal box. As a result of the mixture of rewarded and unrewarded trials, the partially rewarded animal will make these competing responses occasionally on a rewarded trial. Thus, because these competing responses are followed by running to the goal box and being rewarded, the stimuli produced by these competing responses become additional cues for running to the goal box. Presumably, this does not happen to an animal that was rewarded 100 per cent of the time, because it rarely, if ever, makes any competing responses during the training trials. For a partially rewarded animal, therefore, many stimuli that normally would lead to competing behavior, and hence would hasten extinction, have become cues for eliciting the running response. This has not happened for the animal that was always rewarded. For this reason, the partially re-warded animal persists longer during extinction trials than does the animal that was trained on a schedule of 100 per cent reward.

This hypothesis seems plausible, but it is rather difficult to evaluate. The source of the difficulty is the lack of specification of a number of rather important points in the hypothesis, with-out which the hypothesis cannot be tested empirically. Estes (1959) himself admits that application of this theoretical ex-planation to experimental data on extinction "suffers ambiguity because there are no general rules for prescribing just what re-sponses will 'compete' with a given response" (p. 437, note). There are also other vaguenesses and unclarities. There is no specification of any variables that would raise or lower the probability of evoking competing responses during training, and there is no specification of where in the apparatus these compet-ing responses must be evoked in order to produce the increased resistance to extinction.

Let us examine an experiment by Katz (1957) that seems relevant to this explanation. Katz trained rats on two runways simultaneously. These runways were of equal length but other-wise quite distinguishable. Training continued for 10 days, with runs on Alley I and Alley II alternating on each day. The time interval between an animal's run on Alley I and its succeeding run on Alley II was 20 seconds. There was, on the other hand, a 15-minute interval between an animal's run on Alley II and its next run on Alley I. All animals were given 74 acquisition trials on each of the two alleys, and then all were extinguished only on Alley II. Three different conditions of training were employed: (1) One group of animals was rewarded on every trial in both alleys. We shall refer to this as the "100 per cent reward condition." (2) A second group received partial reward (50 per cent) on Alley I, but on the alley used for extinction (Alley II) this group also received 100 per cent reward. We shall refer to this group as the "partial–100 per cent reward con-dition." (3) The third group received 100 per cent reward on Alley I, but on the alley used for extinction (Alley II) this group received 50 per cent reward. To emphasize the experience on the alley used during extinction, we shall refer to this group as the "partial reward condition."

Katz's purpose was to assess the general importance of intertrial versus intratrial effects on resistance to extinction. If intertrial effects are important, then the "partial–100 per cent" group should show the greatest resistance to extinction. For these animals, any unrewarded trial on Alley I was immediately followed by a rewarded trial on Alley II. This arrangement should maximize the possibility that the "partial–100 per cent" group was running to rewards when dominated by the aftereffects of non-reward. On the other hand, what would be expected if increased resistance to extinction in partial reward situations results from intratrial effects, that is, effects occurring specifically on the unrewarded trials? The "partial reward" group was the only one that experienced partial reward on the alley on which extinction trials were run. Hence, if increased resistance to extinction results from something that happens during the unrewarded trial, and independently of the carryover of the aftereffect of an unrewarded to a succeeding rewarded trial, the "partial reward" group should be more resistant to extinction. The results of this experiment are clear. They show that the "partial reward" group is significantly more resistant to extinction than either of the other two. Thus, Katz concludes that intratrial, rather than intertrial, processes are primarily involved in partial reward effects. What implications exist here for the competing response hypothesis?

Let us make some reasonable specifications of the Estes hypothesis with respect to this experiment. Consider the "partial–100 per cent" group that was partially rewarded on Alley I and always rewarded on Alley II. It seems reasonable to assume that these animals would be very likely to make competing responses when run in Alley II. After all, every unrewarded trial in Alley I is immediately followed by a trial in Alley II. Thus, if the occurrence of an unrewarded trial increases the likelihood of competing responses on the very next trial, the training sequence for the "partial–100 per cent" group has maximized competing responses in Alley II. Also, one can be certain that every time a competing response does occur in Alley II it is followed by reward since these animals are always rewarded in Alley II. Undoubtedly the animals make a discrimination between the two alleys, but it seems reasonable to suppose that there is sufficient generalization between them to keep the probability of competing responses in Alley II fairly high.

What would one expect from the "partial reward" group that was always rewarded in Alley I and partially rewarded in Alley II? Here again, of course, one would expect competing responses to occur in Alley II. It must be remembered, however, that immediately preceding any trial in Alley II these animals experienced a rewarded trial in Alley I. Consequently, it is reasonable to assume that the probability of such competing responses would not be too high. In addition, even when competing responses did occur in Alley II, they did not always occur on rewarded trials, since only half of the trials in Alley II were rewarded for this group.

If the above analysis is reasonable, what would one expect concerning differences in the resistance to extinction between these two groups? If one emphasizes the effect of the immediately preceding trial, one would come to the conclusion that the "partial–100 per cent" group should be somewhat more resistant to extinction. If one emphasizes the discrimination that the animal probably develops between the two alleys, one would conclude that those that were partially rewarded in Alley II should be somewhat more resistant to extinction. With these two factors working in opposite directions, any reasonable application of the Estes explanation does not lead one to expect any great difference between these two groups.

The data, however, show a very large difference between these two conditions. Those animals that were partially rewarded on Alley II are very much more resistant to extinction than those partially rewarded on Alley I. Indeed, the latter group is only slightly more resistant to extinction than were the animals that had received 100 per cent reward on both alleys. Thus, if our specifications are reasonable, the data do not support the competing response interpretation. Some readers might argue against the reasonableness of the specifications we have made in trying to apply this interpretation to experimental data. All we can say is that these specifications seem reasonable to us.

Clearly, we have not refuted the existing explanations based upon the concept of competing responses. All we have done is to point to some difficulties in evaluating these explanations. Later in this book we shall return to this problem in connection with some new data that seem directly pertinent.

*The Logan Hypothesis.*—It is quite possible that an unrewarded trial has psychological effects other than the kind emphasized by Sheffield and by Weinstock. For instance, such a trial might change the motivational state of the animal, and this in turn might well produce differences in performance between continuously and partially rewarded animals.

Logan (1960) has attempted to account for the effect of partial rewards along such motivational lines. His account also has the advantage of explicitly dealing with the effects of both partial reward and delay of reward on resistance to extinction. Logan tends to think of the two as being on the same continuum. An unrewarded trial on a partial schedule is, to him, an infinite delay of reward. Consequently, the same explanation should hold for both.

Logan assumes that, when an animal runs and finds food in the goal box, it makes a characteristic set of goal reactions—chewing movements and the like. These goal reactions become anticipatory on later trials. The animal begins to make them as soon as it is placed in the start box. For Logan, it is the arousal of these that provides "incentive motivation." To account for the rapid extinction of continuously rewarded animals, he assumes that when these animals first find an empty goal box, the stimuli present still tend to evoke these goal reactions. During extinction, however, these reactions weaken because they are never followed by reward. It is the extinction of these anticipatory goal reactions, and thus the decrease in the accompanying "incentive motivation," that causes the animal to run more slowly on successive extinction trials.

Logan then accounts for the effect of partial reward and delay of reward on resistance to extinction in the following way. He argues that under these training procedures, the animal has frequent experiences of running into the goal box when food is absent. Gradually, the animal builds up a discrimination that inhibits the tendency to make goal responses when the food is absent. On extinction trials, such an animal has very little tendency to make these goal reactions to the empty goal box. Consequently, these anticipatory goal reactions and the accompanying incentive motivation extinguish very slowly.

In many ways this explanation is very similar to the suggestion made by Mowrer (1960) concerning adaptation to frustration effects. However, Logan's greater specification of his explanation makes it possible to attempt an evaluation of his hypothesis. His account of the effects of delay of reward implicitly assumes that the delay takes place in the goal box. It is the empty goal cup that must become the cue for inhibiting the anticipatory goal responses, and the full one the cue for evoking them. Only if the animal has repeatedly experienced both of these situations can it establish a discrimination of the type postulated. But as was pointed out previously (cf. Wike and McNamara, 1957), there have been studies on delay of reward in which the delay occurred in a special compartment prior to the animal's entrance into the goal box. Once these animals entered the goal box, food was immediately present. Clearly this is a situation in which all the cues in the goal box should become conditioned to eliciting the goal reactions in both the delayed and non-delayed groups. There is no occasion for the delayed animals to learn to inhibit these reactions to the stimulus of an empty food dish because they never experience this condition during training. Nonetheless, when extinction is run directly to the goal box with no further delay for either group, the delay of reward effect on resistance to extinction is still present. This result is clearly at variance with what Logan's hypothesis would predict.

Obviously, one such contradiction is not sufficient to justify ignoring this explanation, especially when it is so far the only one that seemingly integrates the data from both partial reward and delay of reward studies. We believe, however, that much of the data we shall present in the following chapters would be difficult to account for using Logan's concepts.

*The Amsel Hypothesis.*—A different motivational approach to the problem of partial reward effects is based on the work of Amsel (1958). Many of the concepts involved were anticipated by Spence (1960, pp. 97 ff.). Amsel, however, was the first to develop the ideas sufficiently so that they could apply to the effects of partial reward on resistance to extinction.

His explanation rests on the notion of a frustration drive. The presence of this drive may be inferred from the behavior of animals in an apparatus consisting of an initial runway leading to a mid-box and a second runway leading from the mid-box to an end box. Animals were run in this apparatus with a food reward in the mid-box on only a fraction of the trials, but with a reward in the end box on every trial. On unrewarded trials in the mid-box, the animals were delayed for a period of time before being released to run the second alley. The main finding was that the running speed in the second alley was greater after unrewarded mid-box experiences than after rewarded ones. Amsel's interpretation assumes that the experience of non-reward produces a specific but implicit response, the frustration response, which in turn gives rise to a specific pattern of stimulation as well as to the motivational state of frustration. This frustration drive is capable of energizing any habit the animal has learned, such as that of running the second alley. Thus, on unrewarded mid-box trials, according to this hypothesis, the animals have a stronger drive state when they run the second alley than they have on rewarded trials.

Amsel uses these concepts in interpreting the partial reward effect as follows. He considers the frustration response to be aroused on each unrewarded trial the animal experiences. Initially, it is aroused only in the goal box where the animal has learned to expect food. But, like other responses, it can become anticipatory, that is, it can be evoked by stimuli that occur prior to the goal box, such as those in the runway and start box of the apparatus. When this frustration response is aroused, it produces its own specific stimulus pattern. Since this stimulus pattern is present when the animal runs, it becomes associated with this overt behavior and, thus, eventually becomes one of the cues for running. It should be noted that this partially rewarded animal also has a higher drive level than a continuously rewarded animal because of the motivational consequences of this frustration response.

As we understand the Amsel hypothesis concerning extinction, animals trained under 100 per cent reward, and then placed on extinction, have this frustration response aroused for the first time. As it becomes anticipatory, two things occur: (1) because the stimulus pattern characteristic of the frustration response has never been associated with the act of running forward, its presence during extinction tends to arouse competing behaviors that hasten extinction; (2) at the same time, the increase in drive level tends to be channeled into these dominant, competing behaviors and thus also hastens the extinction process. On the other hand, partially rewarded animals did continue to run during training trials in spite of occasional unrewarded trials. This permitted the stimulus pattern characteristic of the frustration response to become associated with running. Consequently, when these same stimuli occur during extinction trials, they tend to elicit the running response rather than competing behaviors. This in itself tends to increase resistance to extinction. At the same time, the frustration drive should help maintain the running behavior.

To the extent that one considers the stimulus functions of this frustration response, the resulting explanation of partial reward effects is not much different from that based on competing responses. Both emphasize that the greater resistance to extinction shown by partially rewarded animals stems from the fact that they have been trained to run to stimuli that are also characteristic of the extinction situation. However, Amsel also invokes a motivational principle to augment the effects attributable to the association between the frustration stimuli and the running behavior. In this respect there is a similarity to the Logan hypothesis. An evaluation of the adequacy of the Amsel hypothesis in accounting for partial and delayed reward effects is difficult at present because of the paucity of relevant experiments. We shall attempt such an evaluation in later chapters in terms of our own research findings.

In this brief review, we have been unable to do justice to all the ingenuity that has been displayed in attempts to account for partial reward and delay of reward effects. It should be clear, however, that there is a great family resemblance among many of the explanations that can be traced back to the discrimination hypothesis. Most of them postulate a greater stimulus similarity between the training and extinction situations for the partially rewarded animal than for the continuously rewarded one. As a consequence, the partially rewarded animal during training forms an association between those stimuli characteristic of the extinction situation and the response of running. This association does not occur for the continuously rewarded animal, and since it does not, the former continues to run during extinction whereas the latter faces a somewhat new and novel stimulus situation that disrupts its performance. The major shift in these accounts over the years has been from an emphasis on intertrial sources of stimulation, as in the Sheffield account, to a reliance on intratrial factors such as frustration responses and competing behaviors.

The one new and stimulating approach to the explanation of partial reward effects has been the introduction of motivational in addition to associational concepts. Our own solution to this theoretical problem, which we shall outline in Chapter 2, also emphasizes the role of motivation. The nature of the motivational concepts we suggest, as well as the manner of their operation in increasing resistance to extinction, is, however, quite different from that suggested by either Logan or Amsel.

# 2

# Dissonance Reduction Effects in Learning Situations

In Chapter 1 we considered the difficulties that learning theory is having at present with a large body of empirical data. Let us briefly review the problem posed by the data:

1. Although rewards are supposed to strengthen a habit, one finds that habits that have been partially rewarded are more resistant to extinction than those that have been continuously rewarded.

2. Although temporal delay between performing a response and obtaining a reward is supposed to weaken a habit, one finds that habits that have been acquired with delayed reward are more resistant to extinction than those acquired without delay.

3. Although expenditure of effort in the performance of a response is supposed to build up inhibition and thus weaken the habit, one finds that habits acquired under conditions requiring considerable effort are more resistant to extinction than those acquired with little expenditure of effort.

We have discussed the inadequacies of the attempts to reconcile this conflict between learning theory and data. In this chapter we shall propose an explanation that we feel is more adequate. We shall begin our presentation by regarding the data from a purely empirical point of view. The reason for doing this is to find some unifying theme running through this diversity of data. If we can do this, we will be closer to finding a theoretical explanation.

## An Empirical Generalization

If one searches for factors common to the three variables of partial reward, delay of reward, and effort, one is impressed by one obvious similarity. This similarity is readily apparent when we consider the animal's reactions in a free choice situation. If an animal is given a choice between an alternative that provides 100 per cent reward and one that provides partial reward, it chooses the 100 per cent rewarded alternative; if given a choice between an alternative where reward is immediate and one where it is delayed, it chooses the immediately rewarded alternative; and if given a choice between two alternative paths to the same goal which differ only in the amount of work required, it chooses the least effortful path. Clearly each of these three variables—partial reward, delay of reward, and effort—is something the animal will avoid if given an opportunity to do so. This contention is easy to support with experimental evidence.

1. *Partial reward.*—Brunswik (1939) reports an experiment in which rats were given a series of learning trials in a T-maze. One arm led to a goal box in which food was always available. The other arm led to a similar goal box in which food was available on only 50 per cent of the trials. The animals quickly learned to go to the side offering 100 per cent rewards significantly more often than chance would allow. When the reward percentages in the two goal boxes were reversed, the animals quickly reversed their behavior. Clearly, animals would rather go to a place where they are always rewarded than to one where they are rewarded only occasionally.

2. *Delay of reward.*—Logan (1952) reports an experiment in which rats were given a choice between two alternatives, both of which led to an equal reward on each trial. For one alternative, the reward appeared one second after the choice was made. If the other alternative was chosen, however, the animal had to wait five seconds before the reward was presented. The data show that the animals quickly learned to choose the alternative that yielded the more immediate reward—they went almost 100 per cent of the time to the alternative where food was presented

after only one second. Furthermore, if after they had learned this, the delay intervals were reversed between the two alternatives, the animals quickly changed their choice. In short, they clearly preferred an immediate to a delayed reward.

3. *Work or effort.*—Numerous studies have shown that rats will choose the shorter of two paths to a goal box. It is not easy, however, to find studies in which the variable of effort is not confounded with other variables, such as the time elapsing between the choice point and the reward. Fortunately, Thompson (1944) reports one experiment in which the alternatives available to the animal did differ only in the amount of effort required. This was achieved by providing a lever that the animal had to press in order to gain access to the reward. One lever required a pressure of forty grams, the other of sixty grams. When given free choice trials, the animals soon learned to choose the low effort alternative on practically every trial, thus showing a marked preference for the less effortful alternative.

Considering these facts about free choice behavior in conjunction with what we already know about resistance to extinction, we can state an empirical generalization of broad scope: *The set of conditions that an animal chooses least often in a free choice situation will result in increased resistance to extinction, in a non-choice situation, if the animal has experienced them during acquisition.* In other words, consider two values of any variable—for example, a long and a short delay of reward. Assume that, in a free choice situation, the animal consistently chooses one in preference to the other when all other things in the situation are equal. This variable, then, should make a difference in resistance to extinction for animals trained in a non-choice situation such as a simple runway. A group that experiences the less preferred value of the variable during training will be more resistant to extinction.

Later we shall have to qualify this generalization, but for the moment let us accept its correctness as stated. The acceptance of this generalization permits us to restate the problem which requires theoretical explanation. We need no longer be concerned with the specificities of partial reward, delay of reward, or effort. Rather, the problem to be explained may be stated as follows: Why does an animal that has been induced to experience repeatedly a less preferred situation show increased resistance to extinction?

## Overview of Dissonance Theory

Stating the problem in this manner suggests that we might find a solution to it by turning to a theory that was developed to account for similar phenomena in humans. This is the theory of cognitive dissonance, initially formulated by Festinger (1957). The theory, in part, deals with situations in which an individual's actions are not entirely consistent with what he knows about the environment. An animal that suffers, say, delay of reward but still continues to run is in a situation where it knows things that are inconsistent with its actions. Since there is some similarity here, perhaps the theory of dissonance can offer an adequate explanation of our empirical generalization. We shall first present a brief, intuitive sketch of the theory as it applies to humans. We shall then develop its implications more rigorously as it applies to resistance to extinction in non-verbal animals.

The theory of cognitive dissonance deals, in part, with the psychological states that arise in humans as a result of taking some action and then finding that the consequences of this act are not sufficient to justify the action taken. Such conditions set up a motivational state called dissonance. Illustrations of situations that might establish dissonance are easy to come by. For instance, there is the new and eager Ph.D. who decides to accept a position at Jones College. After arriving with bag and baggage for the fall term, he finds that the college is very inferior intellectually, socially, and financially. Or again there is the conscientious saver who, after extensive house hunting, buys one and then finds it is riddled by termites, has a leaky roof, and needs new plumbing. In both of these situations dissonance exists. The basis for this dissonance is the opposition between two cognitions, or two sets of information, the individual has. In the latter example, the information that he has purchased the house is dissonant with the information he has about undesirable aspects of the house. Considering *only* things like its ter-

mites and its plumbing, he would not ordinarily have undertaken this action. More generally, dissonance exists between
two pieces of information if the obverse of one would normally
follow from the other for that given individual.

These states of dissonance are said to have motivational
properties because they are tensional systems that the individual
tends to reduce. Such reduction, however, can take place in only
one of two ways. The most common form of dissonance reduction is a change in behavior. If the homeowner were immediately to sell his house to someone else, his new behavior would
be consonant or compatible with his information about the undesirable aspects of its condition. However, it is frequently
impossible to reduce dissonance by such a change of behavior
because of social, financial, or other similar pressures. The homeowner may well be stuck with his lemon. Under these conditions, there is an alternative way in which the individual can
reduce the unpleasant state of dissonance, at least to some degree. He can change his cognition or information about the
consequences of being the owner of the house. This can be done
in a variety of ways. By and large, however, they all involve
seeking additional information that is consonant with the act
of owning the house. He may convince himself that the splen-
did view, the excellent neighbors, and the nearness to schools
and shops more than compensate for the sad state of disrepair.
Or the consonant information he seeks may take even more
subtle forms—the "do-it-yourself" skills he must now acquire
are morally good as well as a benefit to one's health. The exact
form that this type of dissonance reduction will take is difficult
to specify, for it depends to such a large extent on the peculi-
arities of the individual and on the possibilities for finding such
dissonance-reducing information in a given situation.

An alternative way of stating this form of dissonance reduction is to say that the individual sets about discovering values
or rewards in the situation that satisfy some motivation he may
have other than the motivation that led him to take the action
in the first place. In buying a house, the individual was primarily interested in providing an economical and comfortable
shelter for his family. With the arousal of dissonance, however,

the emphasis shifted to other motivations, such as those involved in valuing neighborliness and the like. In the absence of dissonance, these new values and rewards might not have been sought or discovered. But once they have been discovered, they partially reduce the dissonance by giving additional justification for the action taken. At the same time they are now available to influence future actions.

An example of this type of dissonance reduction in humans is illustrated in an experiment by Aronson and Mills (1959). The subjects in their study were college girls who volunteered to join discussion groups. In one experimental condition the girls were allowed to obtain membership in the group very easily. In another condition they were subjected to a rather painful and embarrassing selection procedure before they were admitted. All subjects in both conditions had identical experiences once they became members of the group. The results of the experiment showed clearly that those subjects who had endured unpleasantness in order to be admitted liked the group better and thought the discussions more interesting than did those who gained admission easily. In keeping with the theory, those individuals who engaged in an action involving considerable unpleasantness found additional values in the situation that were not apparent to others.

As applied to humans, this theory of cognitive dissonance is not only plausible but is well documented by experimental evidence. The question remains, however, whether it can be formulated so as to apply to the behavior of a non-verbal animal when it is confronted with partial reward, delayed reward, or effort-evoking situations. We are assuming that these are unpleasant affairs and that when an animal voluntarily engages in an action which involves them, a state of dissonance is aroused. If this is true, the animal can reduce the dissonance by changing its behavior and refusing to repeat this action. If, however, it is induced to continue in this activity (perhaps by being given food when it is hungry), does the animal reduce its dissonance by finding extra attractions in the situation? If it does, this might well account for the increased resistance to extinction that is shown under these training conditions. In light of what we know about human behavior, this type of explanation has considerable face validity. But a satisfactory test of the adequacy of dissonance theory as an explanation for the empirical generalization we stated previously is only possible if the implications of the theory are spelled out somewhat more rigorously. This we shall do in the following section.

*Definition of Dissonance*

Let us specify three types of relationship that can exist between items of information. These are the following:

1. If A psychologically implies B, or B psychologically implies A, then A and B are in a *consonant relationship*.
2. If A psychologically implies not-B, or B psychologically implies not-A, then A and B are in a *dissonant relationship*.
3. If there is no psychological implication at all from A to B, or from B to A, then A and B are in an irrelevant relationship.
    We are, of course, making a number of assumptions about the nature of these psychological implications. For instance, we are assuming that, if A psychologically implies not-B, it is impossible that B psychologically implies A.

Our main concern is with the second item above, the dissonant relationship. It also can be stated somewhat differently: two items of information are in a dissonant relationship if, considering only these two items, the obverse of one follows psychologically from the other. As an illustration, assume that a rat has two items of information resulting from its actual experience. Item A is that it has just run the alley, and item B is that no reward is present. Further, assume that if, at the beginning of the trial, the rat had the information that no reward was present (item B), this would psychologically imply for the rat that it would not run the alley on that trial (not-A). Thus item B psychologically implies not-A, and the rat's information that it has run the alley (item A) is therefore in a dissonant relationship with the information that no reward is obtained (item B).

For the above definition of a dissonant relationship to have precise meaning, it is necessary for us to specify exactly what is meant by psychological implication. This is to be interpreted as follows: if the acceptance of one item of information as true sets up an expectation that some other item of information is also true, then the first item psychologically implies the second. Such psychological implication is, of course, different from logical implication. There are many bases other than logical reasoning for setting up expectations.

Similarly, we need to say something about our usage of the term "item of information," especially as it applies to non-verbal organisms. Nothing very elaborate is intended. We assume that the animal has information about an event, such as the presence or absence of food, whenever that event can be shown to influence its behavior. With this usage, it is clear that it has information both about the consequences of an act it has performed and about the act itself. It is easy to show that its present behavior is determined in part by the action it has just completed.

Such conceptual definitions concerning relationships between items of information, even if stated precisely, are not useful unless one can relate them to the empirical world. We must therefore face the problem of how to determine which items of information have psychological implications for which other items, and we must be able to do this for any given organism. In a like sense, we must be able to determine which items of information an organism possesses at any given time. A complete determination of this sort would, of course, demand an operational method of measurement that would map out all the items of information an organism possesses, and all of the interrelationships among these items. This we cannot give. We can propose, however, operations that will do this for the kinds of information with which we are here concerned. We are primarily interested in only two types of information, that about an action undertaken and that about its consequences.

To illustrate the problem concretely we shall choose, as an example, the question of whether there is any psychological implication, in one direction or the other, between the information that a given course of action inevitably involves some unpleasantness and the information that an organism engages in this behavior. We wish to emphasize, so as not to exaggerate the importance of effort or unpleasantness in the reader's mind, that absence of reward when the person has been oriented toward it or delay of reward would be equally serviceable illustrations.

With a human subject, we could simply ask the following question: "If the only thing you know about a given action is that it involves pain and embarrassment, would you or would you not engage in that action?" We can be reasonably certain that our subject would tell us that he would not. Some subjects, of course, would say that it would depend on other things such as the rewards to be obtained and the possible alternatives. But if we insisted upon knowing the expectation engendered solely by the given piece of information, we would undoubtedly obtain the answer we have suggested. From this we could conclude that for the specific person involved there was a psychological implication between the two items of information, and we would know the direction of the implication. We would be able to say that for this person the information that a given behavior involves pain is consonant with *not* engaging in the action and is dissonant with engaging in it.

But how do we get an answer to this question from a nonverbal animal such as the white rat? Clearly, we must observe its behavior and make some plausible inferences from this observation. For instance, we could give an animal a choice between two arms of a T-maze. If the animal turned right, it would find food with no difficulty. If it turned left, it would also find food but only after considerable difficulty and harassment. Let us assume that, before being given this free choice, the animal had considerable experience with both of the alternatives. Under these circumstances the animal undoubtedly would choose the right turn, that is, the easy alternative. We could then infer that for this animal, considering only the information that a given course of action leads to difficulty and harassment, this psychologically implies that it does not engage in that action.

Such an inference is almost justified, but not quite. It seems justified when we are dealing with conditions that produce pain or difficulty because our intuitive appraisal of the situation fits with such an inference. Consider, however, a comparison that might be made in the same apparatus between a small and a large quantity of food. All other things being equal, a hungry rat undoubtedly would choose the alternative that led to the larger amount of food. In this case we would be unwilling to infer that the information that a given action leads to a small amount of food psychologically implies that the rat does not engage in that action. Thus, the observation of such choices is not sufficient for making this inference. Additional observations are needed. In order to justify our inference we also need evidence that the variable in question (harassment, food, etc.) is a deterrent to action and not an incentive for it.

Suppose that a hungry animal is taught to run a simple straight alley for food reward. After its running behavior has become stabilized, we can introduce an increment of one of the factors under consideration and observe its effects. If we introduce an increment of delay, we have every right to expect that this will slow up, if not prevent, the running behavior. In this sense, delay is a deterrent to action. Indeed, any variable which, when increased in magnitude, makes for decreased willingness to perform an action, may be viewed as a deterrent. This type of observation, in conjunction with the observation of choice behavior, justifies the inference that the animal's information that an action leads to some consequence such as delay psychologically implies that it does not engage in that action. On the other hand, if we add a small increment to the amount of food in our runway situation there is no reason to expect that the animal's willingness to run would decrease. Instead it would probably increase. Thus, we can assert that even small increments of food are an incentive for action, certainly not a deterrent to it. Consequently, in spite of observations of choice behavior between large and small amounts of food, we cannot infer that information that an action leads to a small quantity of food psychologically implies for the animal that it does *not* engage in that activity.

Thus, from these two types of observation we have usable operational specification of when psychological implication holds between information about an action and information about its consequences. We also can determine in this way whether the relationship between the two items of information is a consonant or a dissonant one. Expecting non-reward is consonant with not running and dissonant with running. The converse is true for an incentive factor such as food. There are, of course, many variables that would have no influence on behavior in either the choice or runway situations. In our terminology, none of these would have psychological implication for the action involved. Such variables bear an irrelevant relationship to the behavior under consideration.

We now proceed to examine what we can say, according to these conceptual and operational definitions, about experiences of partial reward, delay of reward, and effort expenditure. Does information that an action leads to any of the above consequences psychologically imply that the animal does not engage in that action? Earlier in this chapter we presented some evidence that animals will choose 100 per cent reward rather than partial reward, immediate reward rather than delayed reward, and the less effortful rather than the more effortful action. The remaining problem is to determine whether or not these are also deterrents to action.

There is little or no problem in connection with delay of reward. Experiments reported in the literature indicate that, as the temporal interval between action and reward increases, the animal performs more slowly (Logan, 1960). Consequently, we can infer that information about enforced delay before obtaining a reward is dissonant with engaging in the action.

In the case of effort or work, the evidence is also reasonably clear cut. As effort is increased, performance becomes poorer (Applezweig, 1951). Here, however, there is some slight ambiguity. Changing the work requirements of a task frequently changes the characteristics of the act that the animal must perform. As a result, a measure such as time may confound the animal's willingness to perform and the time actually needed to perform the act. Nonetheless, we can feel quite certain that information about this work requirement is dissonant with engaging in the action.

In the case of partial reward, the determination of whether or not a dissonant relationship exists is somewhat more difficult, at least at the conceptual level. Training procedures involving partial reward always consist of a mixture of rewarded and unrewarded trials. As we have indicated previously, finding food on rewarded trials is certainly consonant with performing the given action, and therefore any dissonant relationships must stem primarily from the unrewarded trials. But it is by no means clear that simply the absence of some specified reward can be considered to be a general deterrent to action. In a sense, the absence of a given type of reward is not something that influences behavior. The absence of reward would have a deterrent effect only if the animal were strongly motivated for a particular reward and were actively seeking it; in other words, for non-reward to introduce dissonance the animal must expect reward.

There is a clear relationship between what we are saying here and the concepts of expectation and disconfirmation of expectation. For our purposes, nothing more is implied than that the present actions of the animal, such as going to and looking into the food cup, permit us to infer that they are largely determined by its past experiences with food in this situation. Granting this, we can say that not finding a reward is dissonant with performing the act only when a motivated animal expects reward.

In summary, our operational definitions permit us to say that partial reward, delayed reward, and effort expenditure, considered as consequences of an act, are in a dissonant relationship with the performance of the act. Consequently, an animal that experiences any of these during training should accumulate considerable dissonance motivation as long as it can be induced to continue in such activity.

## The Magnitude of Dissonance

Thus far we have discussed how to determine whether or not a relationship of dissonance or consonance exists between two items of information. Since the existence of a dissonant relationship gives rise to a motivational state, it is essential that we specify, both conceptually and operationally, the variables that affect the magnitude of this dissonance motivation. Two questions are pertinent here: (1) considering only a single dissonant relationship between two items of information, what determines the magnitude of the dissonance engendered, and (2) considering that any given item of information may have a variety of different relationships with a number of other items of information, what determines the total magnitude of the dissonance associated with this single item? We shall consider each of these questions in turn.

In general, the magnitude of the dissonance that exists between any two items of information in a dissonant relationship is a direct function of the importance to the individual of each of the items. In the present restricted context, we deal primarily with only two types of information, information about an action that has been undertaken and information about the consequences resulting from the action. For the sake of simplicity of presentation, we shall develop the theory as if the importance of the item of information about the action were a constant, regardless of the context in which that action occurs. For this simplified case, the magnitude of dissonance that exists between items of information about an action and the consequence of that action, when these two are in a dissonant relationship, is a direct function of the importance to the animal of the item concerning the consequence.

This principle, of course, says very little until one specifies what is meant by the importance of an item of information. Undoubtedly, any number of factors control this variable of importance, but two of them are of primary concern in the present context. The first involves the actual content of the item of information: information that the consequences of an action involve considerable pain or effort expenditure has more importance than the information that only a little pain or effort is involved. The second of these factors involves the motivational state of the animal, or at least that part of its motivational state which is relevant to the content of the given item of information. It seems reasonable to assume that, if an animal is hungry, information concerning the presence or absence of expected food is of more importance than if the animal is not hungry; or if an animal is very fatigued, information concerning how much effort it must expend is of more importance than if it is not fatigued. In the situations we deal with, the importance of an item can be roughly specified either by the content of the item or by the motivational state of the animal—the hungrier an animal is, the greater is the magnitude of dissonance created when it runs an alley expecting food and fails to find it. Similarly, the longer an animal is delayed in an apparatus before reaching a goal box, the more dissonance is created.

A similar statement may be made concerning the role of importance in consonant relationships. For example, running and obtaining food form a consonant relationship. The item of information about the consequence of the action has a certain degree of importance depending upon the content of that item and the motivational state of the animal. A large amount of food is of greater importance than a small amount, and any given amount of food is of greater importance for a very hungry animal than for one only slightly hungry. Thus, consonant relations also vary in magnitude. This magnitude is a measure of the animal's justification for performing an act and shows up as its willingness to do so.

What we have said so far applies when only two items of information are considered. We must now consider the case in which a given item of information is related to several other items. As an illustration, consider the hungry rat that runs on a given trial in a delay-of-reward situation. The single item of information of immediate concern is that the action has been performed. But several consequences stem from this. First, the animal does obtain a reward. This information is in a consonant relationship with the action performed. At the same time, it experiences an unpleasant delay. This last item of information is in a dissonant relationship with the action. What we seek is some form of a "combination rule" that will permit us to specify the magnitude of the resulting dissonance.

The combination rule we propose is as follows. We sum, not necessarily arithmetically, all the dissonant relations that may exist, each weighted in terms of its importance, and we sum the consonant relationships, each weighted in terms of its importance. The magnitude of the resulting dissonance is then a joint function of these two. We are unwilling to state the exact mathematical function involved, because at the present stage of development this would be pure guesswork. Nonetheless, this function has two properties: (1) When the weighted sum of the dissonant relationships is held constant, the total magnitude of the resulting dissonance decreases as the weighted sum of the consonant relationships increases; and (2) when the difference of the weighted sums of the dissonant and consonant relationships is constant, the total magnitude of the resulting dissonance increases as the weighted sum of the dissonant relationships increases. In other words, the magnitude of the dissonance is a function both of the absolute value of the sum of the weighted dissonant relationships, and of the difference between this and the weighted sum of the consonant relationships.

In any actual empirical situation many items of information may exist that are dissonant with, or consonant with, engaging in an action. Thus, for example, a situation might exist where an animal expends effort, suffers delay, and also, on occasion, does not find food when it expects to. Given our current possibilities for technical measurement, we could not specify which of these dissonant relationships would be greatest or how much each would contribute to the total magnitude of dissonance when "added" together. All we can say is that each of them *would* contribute.

### The Reduction of Dissonance

The core of our formulation is that dissonance is a motivational state. When it exists the animal acts in ways that are oriented toward reducing the magnitude of this dissonance. In the present context, we are concerned only with dissonance between information about an action and about its consequences. In general, there are only two major ways in which this particular dissonance can be reduced. The animal can change its information about its action, or, alternatively, it can change its information about the consequences of the action. We shall discuss each of these in turn.

Consider an animal in a delay-of-reward experiment. It has information that it has run in this situation. This is consonant with the information that it obtains a reward for doing so, but it is dissonant with the information that it must suffer a delay. Consequently, some magnitude of dissonance exists, and this creates tendencies to reduce it. One means of reducing it is for the animal to change its behavior. Assume that there is an alternative route to the goal that does not involve a delay. Choosing this new alternative is consonant with its information that the original path involved a delay. At the same time this new action remains consonant with obtaining the reward. Thus, by changing its behavior, it has reduced all the dissonance. Its new action, which also implies that it refuses to engage in the original one, is now in a consonant relationship with all the information it has about the consequences in the situation.

This tendency to change behavior is usually the most convenient and the most effective way to reduce dissonance. By changing its behavior, the organism can completely reduce dissonance if the new action is (1) consonant with those items of information that were also consonant with the previous action, and (2) converts those items of information that were dissonant with respect to the old action into ones consonant with the new one. Even if a new action does not completely reduce dissonance, change of behavior will occur as long as the dissonance aroused by the new action is less than that stemming from the original one. The greater the variety of possible actions available to an animal in any situation, the greater is the likelihood that it will adopt this method of dissonance reduction.

There are situations, however, in which a change of behavior is not an effective means of reducing dissonance. Again consider the animal in a delay-of-reward situation, but with only one available route to the goal. We shall assume that the weighted sum of the consonant relationships, resulting from the fact that it obtains food, is greater than the weighted sum of the dissonant relationships, resulting from its experiences with the delay. Even under these conditions, considerable dissonance can exist. If the animal now attempts to reduce the dissonance by changing its behavior, the only possibility is to refuse to run. In so refusing, of course, it converts its information about the delay into a consonant relationship with the new behavior. At the same time, however, its information that a reward is available is converted into a dissonant relationship with this refusal to run. If the reward consequence has greater importance for the animal than the delay, this means that the new action results in more dissonance than did the original one. Clearly, under such circumstances, dissonance can *not* be reduced by a change in behavior. Therefore, an animal may continue to engage in a given action even though it actually experiences considerable dissonance, because a refusal to act would result in an even greater amount of dissonance.

The reader will realize that the situations with which we are primarily concerned in this book are precisely of this type, namely, situations in which dissonance cannot be effectively reduced by changing behavior. Experiments on partial reward, delay of reward, and effort are always carefully designed so as to ensure that the animal continues to perform the required action. In terms of our formulation, this means that the procedure has been so rigged that refusing to respond is not an effective way of reducing dissonance.

Consequently, we are particularly concerned with how an organism reduces dissonance when it does not change its behavior. The only remaining way available to it is to change the items of information concerning the consequences of its act. But how does it do this? Conceptually, of course, the possibilities here are clear and delimitable. They are three in number: (1) The animal can reduce the importance of those items of information that are dissonant with the action and increase the importance of those that are consonant with it; (2) it can reinterpret items of information that are dissonant with the action, making them either irrelevant or consonant; and (3) it can make either previously irrelevant or new items of information consonant with its action. Any of these procedures will reduce the magnitude of the dissonance.

The human being has a great capacity for self-delusion and can employ all of these methods. With the help of social support from others, with his freedom to change the realities of his environment, and with his ability to rationalize, the human is an excellent dissonance reducer. We are dealing here, however, primarily with the white rat, presumably a much more reality-bound organism. We simply do not know which, if any, of these various possibilities are available to the rat in reducing dissonance. One thing is perfectly clear, however: a theory involving the concept of dissonance reduction must specify in fairly concrete fashion the mechanism, or mechanisms, by means of which such reduction is achieved. Depending upon which mechanism is specified, there may be different implications for behavior even though the process by means of which dissonance is aroused has been correctly described by us so far.

Partly on our intuitions as to what we believe is possible for the rat, and partly because of the exciting implications for behavior theory, we have chosen to develop a mechanism that provides a basis for making new items of information consonant with behavior. But before discussing this mechanism further, we should like to emphasize that alternative mechanisms are possible.

An animal such as the white rat is not a simple organism. Even when one motivation such as hunger is dominant, it simultaneously has a variety of other drives and motivations. We have no intention of trying to specify these; perhaps normally they are weak and unimportant both to the animal and to the learning theorist. We wish to assume, however, that these subordinate motivations do exist—an assumption that seems quite plausible in terms of what is known, for example, about exploratory, manipulatory, and sensory stimulation needs in animals. Granted this, such subordinate motivations may provide a means by which the animal can reduce dissonance. If it begins to note and pay attention to aspects of the situation that satisfy these other motivations, it is discovering new items of information about the consequences of its action that are consonant with it. Loosely speaking, we can say that the animal has discovered "extra attractions" in the situation. These can be aspects of the action itself, of the apparatus, or of the consequences of its behavior. We cannot specify them any more exactly without knowing which motivations the animal has and what will satisfy them, but we can assert that new attractions of this sort probably are discovered by the animal whenever dissonance occurs and the behavior does not change.

The assumptions made in the above statement should be emphasized. We are asserting that even though an animal has a variety of subordinate motivations, these do not always enter into the determination of its behavior. This is true when most of the items of information concerning the consequences of its act are consonant with it. If the animal is dominated by a strong drive such as hunger, the mere fact of temporal contiguity between the subordinate motivations and their potential satisfiers is not sufficient to relate them. The animal seeks satisfaction of these subordinate motivations, however, if a state of dissonance exists. In this sense, dissonance as a motivational state has a unique property: it acts as a catalyst in relating subordinate motives to satisfiers in a situation where this serves to reduce the dissonance. The implication of this is that an animal that is continuously and immediately rewarded after performing an effortless act will not discover these "extra attractions." An animal that experiences either partial reward, delay of reward, or considerable effort expenditure *will* discover them.

We can summarize this discussion by saying that, when dissonance is created for an animal under conditions in which its behavior does not change, "extra attractions" will develop for it in connection with the activity, the apparatus, or the consequence of the act. This occurs primarily because the pressures to reduce dissonance result in the animal's discovering new aspects of the situation that serve as satisfiers for the variety of other motivations it has at the time.

### The Cumulative Aspects of Dissonance Reduction

Thus far we have discussed the theory of dissonance without regard to any cumulative aspects. While we have defined the conditions that create dissonance and have suggested various means for reducing it, we have largely acted as though all of this occurs on a single occasion. Our primary concern here, however, is with situations of partial reward, delay of reward, and effort, all of which typically involve a large number of repetitive experiences. It is therefore necessary to specify how the state of the animal is affected by repeated experiences with dissonant relationships.

Let us consider a hungry animal that has discovered through experience that it is rewarded with food whenever it engages in a given action. This information about the food reward is consonant with the information that it engages in the action. In the following discussion we shall assume that the weighted sum of the consonant relationships is sufficiently great so that the animal never refuses to act.

What happens to the animal when it first acquires information that there are aspects of the situation that are dissonant with its action? Suppose it finds that it must expend much effort, or that it experiences an enforced delay, or that it fails to obtain food on some occasions. All of these items of information result in some magnitude of dissonance, which the animal attempts to reduce primarily by finding "extra attractions" in the situation. What is the state of the animal after its first experience with this dissonance?

First, consider one extreme of a possible continuum. Conceivably we might have an animal that is extremely adept and effective at reducing dissonance. On the very first occasion it finds so many "extra attractions" that little or no dissonance remains. The human is sometimes capable of this. For example, a human might persuade himself that much exercise before dinner makes the food taste better; that waiting for dinner provides him with the one enjoyable, quiet period of each day; and that occasionally not having dinner at all gives him a better appreciation of the spiritual aspects of life. But even the human cannot usually be so effective at dissonance reduction, and the white rat certainly cannot. However, if an animal were this effective, there would be no cumulative problem to discuss. The next time it experienced the same situation there would be little or no dissonance introduced and therefore, obviously, little to reduce.

At the other end of the continuum there well may be organisms, perhaps quite low in the phylogenetic order, that cannot reduce dissonance in any of the ways we have suggested. For these, also, there is no cumulative problem. They do not find extra attractions in the situation, and thus there is no decrease in the magnitude of the dissonance. Additional experiences do not modify this state of affairs in any way. For such organisms, if our theory is correct, partial reward, delay of reward, and effort expenditure should not enhance resistance to extinction; if anything, they should weaken it. Very little work has been done on the effects of dissonance-producing variables on resistance to extinction in animals that are very low in the phylogenetic order, although there is a suggestion that fish do not show the partial reward effect (Wodinsky and Bitterman, 1959, 1960; Longo and Bitterman, 1960). After initial training, a 100 per cent rewarded group of fish proves more resistant to extinction than a partially rewarded group.

The white rat probably does not fall at either extreme of this continuum. The first time dissonance occurs, it probably is able to reduce only a minute part of the dissonance by finding "extra attractions." Consequently, the next time it encounters the same situation, considerable dissonance is again aroused. Perhaps this time it finds some additional aspects that help reduce dissonance. This continues to occur on successive trials. Thus, for such an animal, we do have to account for a cumulative aspect in dissonance reduction.

It is, of course, quite impossible to state the precise quantitative function that describes the way in which "extra attractions" accumulate with the repeated introduction of dissonance, but we can make a number of plausible specifications for this function. First of all, it is likely that for an animal such as the white rat these attractions build up slowly and continuously as the number of dissonance-producing experiences increases. Furthermore, it seems reasonable to assume that there may be an initial acceleration in the rate of this accumulation. This is based on the hunch that once some "extra attractions" have been discovered, the process becomes easier. It also seems plausible that in any given situation there is a maximum value for the accumulation of these "extra attractions." In the usual experimental situation we are discussing, this maximum is probably a relatively low value.

One factor influencing this maximum is the nature of the situation in which training takes place. If the development of these "extra attractions" depends, as we assume it does, on finding aspects of the activity or situation that act as satisfiers for subordinate motivations, then obviously a limit is placed on this process by what is or is not available to the animal in a given situation. If the environment is rich, in the sense that there are many aspects of it that can satisfy various drives, then the amount of "extra attraction" which could develop is potentially large. This would be most likely if an experimental apparatus were very similar to the natural habitat of the animal involved. If, on the other hand, the experimental situation were rather barren of those aspects that can satisfy subordinate motivations, as is probably true for most of the apparatuses we use, then there would undoubtedly be a relatively low limit placed on the accumulation of these "extra attractions." In this latter case dissonance reduction should have only weak effects on the observed behavior.

A second factor that might be expected to determine the maximum development of "extra attractions" is the strength of the animal's dominant drive. If the animal is extremely hungry, for example, it seems plausible to assume that the subordinate motivations are difficult to activate and that the animal is less capable, psychologically, of discovering things that will satisfy them; on the other hand, the activation and discovery processes might both occur more readily when the animal is only slightly hungry. Thus, we may reasonably assert that the stronger the dominant drive in a given situation, the lower is the maximum level for the development of "extra attractions."

In summary, our formulation implies that, after repeated experiences with a dissonance-arousing situation, the state of the animal is different. In order to reduce the dissonance it has discovered "extra attractions" in the situation that serve to satisfy its subordinate motivations. The accumulative magnitude of these "extra attractions" depends upon the number of dissonance-introducing experiences the animal has had, the richness of its environment, and the strength of the dominant drive. All else being constant, the amount of dissonance introduced on successive occasions decreases as this accumulation process continues.

The discovery of these "extra attractions" clearly adds new

consonant relationships. How much they increase the sum of the weighted consonant relationships depends, of course, upon their importance, and their importance is, in turn, a function of the strength of the subordinate motivations. Although we know little about these motivations, it is plausible that they are relatively numerous and fairly stable. If this is true, then these new consonant relationships should also be relatively stable as long as the newly discovered attractions continue to be available in the situation. The resulting picture of these new consonant relationships is that of an almost intrinsic set of justifications for continuing in the action. Even though their over-all effect on behavior may be weak in any given experiment, they should be relatively enduring.

There are, however, conditions that will decrease the strength of these new attractions, either momentarily or lastingly. The first of these is any change in the situation. It is certainly obvious that any change in the characteristics of the situation may involve the elimination or modification of those aspects that are acting as satisfiers for the subordinate motivations, and thus the elimination of the new consonant relationships as well.

These "extra attractions" can also be weakened or eliminated by changes in the animal's behavior. This is a slightly more complicated process and needs some discussion. It will be recalled that these attractions develop when dissonance is introduced under circumstances where the animal cannot change its behavior. They are a means of reducing this dissonance by providing justification for continuing in that action. What should occur, once these attractions have been developed, if the animal is now induced to change its behavior? Such a change in behavior can be brought about in two ways: (1) The experimenter can remove the original rewards in the situation, for example, the food, as in extinction trials. This does not affect the "extra attractions" the animal has developed, but it does reduce the weighted sum of the consonant relationships sufficiently so that the animal may now further reduce its dissonance by changing its behavior. (2) The experimenter can provide a very attractive alternative to the original action and the original goal, thus allowing the animal to reduce the dissonance by choosing this new alternative instead of continuing its original behavior.

In either case, the information the animal has, that its original action would lead to the "extra attractions," will now be in a dissonant relationship with its new behavior. One way in which this new dissonance can be reduced is for the animal to weaken the newly developed "extra attractions." Thus, any factor in the situation which induces the animal not to engage in the action in which it has been trained can be expected to start a process that is the reverse of the development of "extra attractions."

In summary, we can expect the "extra attractions" that develop in a situation, as the result of dissonance reduction, to be stable and long enduring under normal circumstances. They can be weakened or eliminated, however, if either the situation is changed or the animal is induced not to engage in the original behavior.

## Implications for Behavior During Acquisition

The previous sections have defined the conditions under which dissonance occurs and the means by which it can be reduced. We shall now relate these processes to the observable performance of the animal during training or acquisition trials.

We have already stated that, in the absence of any dissonance, the animal's willingness to perform (as shown by latencies, running times, and similar measures) is a direct function of the weighted sum of all the consonant relationships in the situation. This implies that the hungrier it is or the larger the reward the faster the animal will run. Of course, the greater the dissonance introduced the greater is the decrease in this willingness to perform. The very nature of our operational test situations for determining whether or not given variables introduced dissonance implies this effect on willingness to perform. We must now relate these functions to the progressive changes in willingness to perform that occur as dissonance is created and as it is reduced through the accumulation of "extra attractions" in the situation.

To be as specific as possible, imagine an animal that is trained to run an alley for continuous and immediate reward with relatively little effort demanded. Assuming that the animal is well tamed and adapted before this training begins, it should soon reach a stable level of running. Once this has occurred, imagine that we enforce a delay on each succeeding trial, or else require a greater expenditure of effort. Either of these should introduce dissonance for the first time, and this should result in some unwillingness to run as shown by a decrease in running speed. The animal's performance should change fairly rapidly, but, with the same conditions on every trial, it should then tend to become stabilized at a new value.

The situation is more complicated whenever there is variability in the conditions of training from trial to trial—for example, in partial reward situations. On some trials, the action results in a reward, on others in a non-reward. And these consequences occur in an unpredictable order. The same variability may be present in experiments on delayed reward or effort expenditure when these conditions are introduced on only a proportion of the trials. The result is that the animal can never have complete and certain information at the beginning of a trial of the consequences that will stem from acting on that occasion. With this uncertainty in the information, there is a question as to the amount of variability to expect in the animal's performance on successive trials. Largely on intuitive grounds, we should expect, in a partial reward situation, that each rewarded trial would increase the willingness of the animal to run on the succeeding one. All the consequences of the action on that occasion were consonant with that action. Similarly, we should expect each unrewarded trial to decrease this willingness because of the dissonant consequences encountered. The result should be more fluctuations in performance than under conditions where each trial has the same consequences. But in any event, it is clear that, as long as some dissonance is present, animals being trained under either partial reward, delay of reward, or high effort should run more slowly, on the average, than those that receive continuous and immediate reward after little expenditure of effort.

The above statement that under stable training conditions even animals with dissonance will reach a stable performance level needs some qualification. Each trial provides them with an opportunity to discover "extra attractions" in the situation. As these accumulate, the weighted sum of the consonant relationships increases, with a corresponding decrease in total magnitude of dissonance. Consequently, their performance should gradually improve. The differences in performance between these animals and those run without dissonance would diminish or even disappear with continued training if the conditions of acquisition permit a large accumulation of "extra attractions." In fact, it is theoretically possible, under the present formulation, that the order of performance in these two groups could be reversed in circumstances where "extra attractions" can be developed very readily. This, however, would undoubtedly be a rare finding.

## Implications for Resistance to Extinction

We now come to the point of considering the implications of this formulation for measures of resistance to extinction. Imagine two groups of animals, an experimental group trained to engage in an action under conditions where dissonance was created and a control group trained comparably except that dissonance was never introduced. At the end of acquisition, these two groups differ in at least one important aspect: the experimental group has gradually developed "extra attractions" that are consonant with the action involved, while the control group has not. Extinction trials are now begun. This means that the experimenter removes from the situation all the rewards that initially induced the animals to perform the act. In essence, he removes all the consequences that are consonant with running which are held in common by the two groups. He does not, however, remove any of those features that are the source of "extra attractions" for the experimental group.

Let us now consider what happens to the control group that never experienced dissonance. As extinction trials continue, these animals learn that food is no longer available, and as their certainty of this increases, they should become less and less willing to run even though their motivation remains high. Of course, their first discovery that rewards are no longer present not only begins a process of change in their knowledge about the consonant relationships in the situation, but it also gives them their first inkling that it contains dissonant relationships. When this dissonance exists, the animal will attempt to reduce it. Whether the dissonance occurs on trials that the experimenter calls "acquisition" or "extinction" is irrelevant; the dissonance can still be reduced in either of two ways. (1) The animal can convert the consequence of the act into something that justifies the action. This is the procedure of finding "extra attractions" in the situation. (2) The animal can change its behavior so that it becomes consonant with the consequence that was experienced—meaning, in the present case, that it would refuse to run. Here, however, there is a crucial difference between "acquisition" and "extinction" trials.

As we have pointed out previously, the animal cannot employ behavior change as a mode of dissonance reduction as long as its expectations of finding food are strong and it is highly motivated for such reward. To refuse to run under these circumstances would produce more dissonance than to continue to run. These are the circumstances characteristic of "acquisition" trials. "Extinction" trials, however, are different in principle in that the animal will be able to reduce dissonance effectively by not running. It is true that, during the first trials of extinction, while its certainty of finding a reward is still relatively great, it should continue in the learned behavior, and the resulting dissonance would tend to reduce itself, in so far as this is possible, by the discovery of "extra attractions." Such a process is, however, relatively slow and gradual. Meanwhile, the animal's repeated experiences with this extinction situation have altered its certainties about what to expect as a consequence of running. In essence, there has been a decrease in the weighted sum of the consonant relationships and a corresponding increase in the weighted sum of dissonant ones. At some point in this process, it is clear that by refusing to run the animal will experience less dissonance as a consequence of its new behavior than if it persisted in the old running response. It is at this point that the procedure of behavioral change becomes the dominant mode of reducing dissonance.

This account of extinction in a control animal is relatively imprecise and must remain so until we are willing to express the relationships involved in a much more quantitative way. But even at this descriptive level it is clear that extinction should be relatively rapid for an animal that has never experienced dissonance during acquisition. The process hinges largely on two factors: first, there is a change in the animal's knowledge or certainty about the consonant and dissonant relationships that are experienced in the situation; and second, there is an arousal of dissonance under circumstances where it can be effectively reduced by a change in behavior.

With this picture of the control animal in mind, we now turn to the performance of the experimental animal during extinction trials. As a result of its training, this animal starts the extinction trials with an extensive background of dissonance experiences. This training has been of such a nature that the only mode of dissonance reduction available has been the discovery of "extra attractions"; behavior change was not possible. These "extra attractions" are not removed during extinction trials. Thus, while the control animal receives no reward at all when extinction trials start, the experimental animal continues to enjoy its "extra attractions."

The initial trials of extinction should also produce gradual changes in its certainties about the consequences that follow the act of running just as in the case of the control animal. There should be a decrease in the weighted sum of consonant relationships and a corresponding increase in the weighted sum of dissonant ones as these relate to knowledge about the extrinsic reward. Thus, one would expect a decrease in willingness to run, but this decrease should not be of the same magnitude as for the control animals in that the experimental animals still have consonant relations stemming from the "extra attractions."

The experimental animals do, however, experience dissonance on each of the extinction trials. The magnitude of this dissonance would not be as great as that experienced by the control animals, but the experimental ones should still attempt to reduce it. The central question is, at what point during extinction will the gradual changes that are taking place in the weighted sums of the consonant and dissonant relationships have reached the stage where the animal can reduce the dissonance more by changing its behavior than by persisting in the old activity? Many factors would have to be taken into account to give an answer to this question. The rate of continued development of "extra attractions," the rate at which information about the absence of food is acquired, the initial strength of the "extra attractions," and the motivations of the animal—all are relevant. Different assumptions would lead to different precise answers to the question. Whatever the precise answer might be, however, it is clear that, because of the "extra attractions," the experimental animals will take longer than the controls to reach a point where refusing to run becomes dominant. Indeed, a refusal to run at any stage of extinction should tend to produce more dissonance in the experimental animal than in the control animal.

Theoretically, as we have indicated earlier, the point at which the animal refuses to run might never be reached if the "extra attractions" developed during training were of such a magnitude that the experimental animal experienced little dissonance when it performed the act. This outcome would be a rare occurrence indeed considering the limitations placed on the development of "extra attractions" by the characteristics of the situation, the presence of a dominant motive, and similar factors. But even in our usual experimental situations, the arousal of dissonance during training should make for a measurable increase in persistence during extinction.

Granting once more that our formulation is still largely nonquantitative, nonetheless we believe we have stated it precisely enough for the reader to understand the processes we envisage and their interrelationships. The real test of the formulation, however, is whether it can give a coherent account of the data available on partial reward, delay of reward, effort expenditure, and other dissonance-producing procedures. Even more important is the question of whether its implications lead us to new phenomena and relationships that have not been suggested by other formulations. In succeeding chapters, we shall attempt to show that both of these criteria are met by presenting a considerable amount of new experimental data and by relating these findings to the existing literature.

# 3

# Evidence for the Development
# of Attractions

At a gross level the empirical data that have been mentioned
in the previous chapters are consistent with the theory of dissonance. This is not surprising since, if it were not so, it would
never have occurred to us to apply the theory of dissonance to
them. What we need now is a more extensive look at both existing data and new data that bear specifically on derivations
from this theory. It seems sensible first to examine the data
relevant to the basic derivation we have made, namely, that
in the process of reducing dissonance the animal develops a
"liking" for the activity, the place, or some consequence of the
action it undertakes. This derivation is basic in the sense that
it follows most immediately from the theory, and also in the
sense that the other implications concerning resistance to extinction follow from it. The question before us, then, is whether
the experimental data support this derivation. Do animals, after
repeated experience with partial reward, delay of reward, or
effort expenditure, develop extra attractions in the situation
which are independent of the extrinsic rewards?

On the surface, this would seem to be an easy question to
answer. Indeed, it is, if one is dealing with the verbal human
being. One can ask the subject various questions concerning
"liking" and "attractiveness" both before and after a series of
partial reward experiences and then observe whether or not
"liking" increases. Despite the negative feelings many psychologists have toward these "verbal" responses, this is undoubtedly

the most direct way of measuring changes in the attractiveness of a situation or activity. Aronson (1961), for example, has shown by the use of such questions that humans increase their liking for a color that has been associated with the unrewarded trials in a partial reward sequence.

Despite how one feels about this procedure, however, it remains a fact that it is inapplicable to the non-verbal animal. For a non-verbal animal we are forced to infer the existence of attractions from observation of actions. This problem has been faced repeatedly in connnection with the study of secondary rewards, that is, in attempts to demonstrate that attractions develop through the association of stimuli with primary rewards. The techniques used to demonstrate these secondary reward effects have been mainly of the following types: (1) tests to see if the animal would learn a new behavior rewarded only by the opportunity to get back to the "attractive" situation, (2) preference tests to see if the animal would choose the "attractive" situation over a neutral one, and (3) extinction tests to see if the animal would persist longer in a learned action when the source of "attraction" was present than when it was absent. All of these tests have shortcomings, but since they are the only ones available we shall use them to determine whether similar attractions result from dissonance reduction.

## Learning a New Behavior

The most convincing evidence for the existence of an attraction would come from the demonstration that an animal will learn a new action when the only reward is the availability of these attractions. In order to demonstrate that, as a result of a given set of experiences, some previously neutral set of stimuli has become attractive, two things must be shown: (1) prior to the given experiences the set of stimuli in question did not support learning, and (2) after the experiences, the stimuli do support learning. It is then a plausible inference that these experiences have resulted in the development of some attractiveness. Specifically, in the case of secondary reward studies, the animal usually has been trained to run an alley in order to find food in a goal box. The alley has then been removed and the animal is required to perform some new action, such as bar pressing, in order to gain access to the goal box, which is now empty. It is usually known or assumed that the animal would not learn to press the bar in order to gain entrance to the empty box if the box had never been associated with food. If, then, the animal does learn and maintain this bar-pressing behavior, we conclude that the association of the box with reward during the initial training has resulted in the box itself becoming attractive.

The main difficulty of such a procedure is that it is very insensitive to small degrees of attractiveness. In order to provide a test situation, a totally different type of action is required of the animal in the test than was required during training. But this means that many aspects of the training apparatus have been changed or eliminated along with their possible contribution to the attractiveness one is trying to measure. It is probably for this reason that this procedure has provided very little evidence for secondary reward (Myers, 1958). In the case of attractiveness resulting from dissonance reduction, we also should expect, in the usual laboratory apparatus, a relatively weak effect in the rat. Since part of this weak attractiveness may be associated with the action involved as well as with aspects of the goal box, changes in the activity would further weaken the observable effects. We should thus expect that tests based on new learning would be a very insensitive measure.

There is one outstanding example in the literature where, by combining the effects of secondary reward with the effects of dissonance reduction, good results were obtained. Zimmerman (1957) provides a demonstration of relatively strong and lasting attractiveness by this new learning technique. His general procedure is well illustrated by one of his studies (1959). Animals were trained to run an alley to a goal box under partial reward conditions. The percentage of rewarded trials was gradually reduced as training proceeded until eventually rewards were given but rarely. In terms of our formulation, this means that the number of unrewarded, and thus the number of dissonance-producing trials is very great. To test for attractions that have developed, a lever was inserted into the door of the start box, and the animal had to learn to press it in order to gain access to the whole apparatus. There was, of course, no extrinsic reward present during these test trials. Furthermore, as the test trials proceeded, the animal had to press the lever an increasing number of times in order to open the door. From the point of view of a dissonance reduction formulation, this procedure has two outstanding features: (1) the entire training situation is maintained so that any attractiveness associated with aspects of the running behavior, the alley, or the goal box can influence the animal's desire to gain access to the apparatus; and (2) it confounds possible secondary reward effects with the dissonance reduction features. Under these training and testing conditions, Zimmerman obtains very clear evidence of strong and enduring extra attractions in the situation in which partial reward training has occurred.

The results of these studies are perfectly consistent with what we would expect from dissonance theory, and to that extent they are interesting and encouraging. At the same time, it must be admitted that they are not very helpful from a theoretical point of view. So many variables are confounded in this procedure that it is impossible to determine how much of this attractiveness stemmed from the processes we have emphasized in our formulation. On the other hand, it seems clear that a less confounded, simple test procedure makes it difficult to reveal the existence of extra attractions which may be weak. It appeared possible, however, to add to the evidence concerning such attractions by augmenting them with a small extrinsic reward in a simple new learning situation. If, for example, one could find an extrinsic reward which in itself was insufficient to produce or maintain new learning, it could be added to the attractions developed through dissonance reduction. If this combination produced clear-cut learning, we would then be justified in concluding that the initial experiences of the animal had resulted in the development of extra attractions. The following study was designed with this purpose in mind.

*Experiment 1.—The Summation of Extra Attractions and Extrinsic Reward*

The idea behind this experiment was to train one group of rats on a 100 per cent reward schedule and another on a partial schedule, and then to require each group to learn a new task in order to reach the familiar goal box. To facilitate learning of the new task, however, the animals would occasionally find food in the goal box. The frequency of reward during the learning of this new task was intended to be so low that, by itself, it would not produce learning. Thus, if the partially rewarded animals developed stronger attractions in the goal box, as the result of dissonance reduction and secondary reward, than did the 100 per cent animals, as the result of secondary reward alone, the partially rewarded animals would learn the new task more rapidly.

Fifty-two female rats were trained to run a straight, unpainted, 4-foot runway in order to reach a black goal box. The animals were, of course, first tamed and adapted to a 22-hour food deprivation schedule. After 14 preliminary training trials, all of which were rewarded, the animals were divided into two groups matched in terms of their running times. One of these groups, the 100 per cent group, received a reward of a wet mash pellet on each subsequent trial. The other one, the partial reward group, was rewarded on only part of the subsequent trials. All animals were given 6 trials a day for 22 days, or a total of 132 training trials. The partial reward group started these trials on a 50 per cent schedule. As training continued, this per cent of reward was reduced until, on the last 9 days of training, only one of the 6 trials each day was rewarded. Altogether, a partially rewarded animal received only 31 rewards during the 132 trials. The purpose of reducing the reward schedule to a very low figure was to increase the development of extra attractions in the goal box.

Upon completion of this training, all animals were given a new task to learn: they were required to climb over four hurdles, each 4 inches high, in a gray runway 68 inches long. The runway made four right-angled turns—left, right, right, left. The animals received 6 trials a day for 8 days on this new runway. They were permitted 5 minutes on the first 2 trials, 3 minutes on each of the next 4, and only one minute on the remainder to complete a run. If they failed to enter the goal box within these times, they were removed from the apparatus. All animals received the same schedule of reward on this new task. To encourage the animals in the beginning, the first 2 trials were rewarded. Thereafter, the rewards were very sparse, only 5 in the next 46 trials.

Before the start of training on the new task, the 100 per cent reward group and the partial reward group were each divided into two subgroups. Eighteen of the 26 animals in each of these groups had the same goal box for the new task that they were familiar with from the initial task. Thus, any attractions developed in it during initial training should still be effective during the new learning. On the new task, however, the remaining eight animals from each of the groups found a very different goal box, one differing in color, shape, size, and floor texture from the one they had first experienced. These subgroups were essentially controls. If they had developed any attractions for the initial goal box, these should be absent or at least greatly diminished during the new learning.

One animal died during training. The results of a second animal that was run to a new goal box were discarded because it failed to show any learning on the new task. The composition of the four groups is shown in Table 3.1.

TABLE 3.1

DESIGN OF EXPERIMENT ON NEW LEARNING AFTER PARTIAL REWARD
(EXPERIMENT 1)

| Test Condition | Condition of Original Learning | |
| --- | --- | --- |
| | 100 Per Cent Reward | Partial Reward |
| Original goal box with new task | N = 18 | N = 17 |
| New goal box with new task | N = 7 | N = 8 |

Figure 3.1 shows the average running times for each of the four groups during the 48 trials on the new task. Since, with such a low reward schedule, there is considerable fluctuation in these times from trial to trial, the averages are presented for blocks of 12 trials, that is, two consecutive days. On the first 2 trials there were no significant differences among the various groups. It is clear that all groups showed some learning. The fact that the two control groups, those running to a new goal box, also showed learning is evidence that the extrinsic reward we provided was undoubtedly somewhat larger than we had hoped

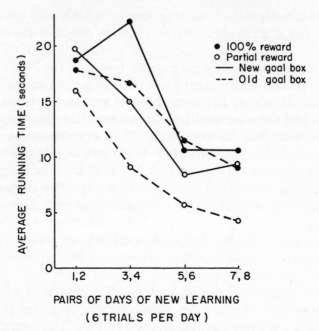

FIG. 3.1.—LEARNING A NEW TASK AFTER PARTIAL AND 100 PER CENT REWARD (EXPERIMENT 1)

for. We must, therefore, examine the rate of learning shown by the experimental groups in comparison to the control groups.

The group trained with a 100 per cent reward schedule, running the new task to the old goal box, does not differ materially in its rate of learning from either of the two control groups. No significant differences exist among them. This would tend to indicate that the effect of secondary reward alone is very slight even when augmented by some extrinsic reward. The slight superiority of the partial reward group over the 100 per cent reward group, when running to a new goal box, is probably due to some generalization of the partial reward effect.

The animals that were partially rewarded during training and encountered the original goal box on the new task show a very different picture. Although starting at the same level as the other groups on the first two trials, the animals in this group improved more rapidly, and on the last two days they averaged 4.2 seconds per trial—quite fast for this task. This value differs from the average of the other three at the .05 level of significance. It would appear from this evidence that some extra attraction did develop in the original goal box as the result of partial reward experiences, and that it was stronger and more enduring than any attraction resulting from being rewarded there on each trial. In other words, the attractions resulting from dissonance reduction and secondary reward are clearly greater than from the latter alone.

Considering the results of this study and those obtained by Zimmerman, we can infer that stronger attractions develop in the goal box during partial reward than during 100 per cent reward training. This is, of course, to be expected in terms of a dissonance reduction theory. Nonetheless, we must admit that, at best, these extra attractions are rather weak as measured by this new learning technique. Our conclusions would carry greater weight if the same effect could be demonstrated by other procedures. With this in mind, let us look at the results that have been obtained using preference tests.

## Choosing Between Alternatives

Offhand, a choice or preference procedure for determining relative attractiveness appears to be very simple and straightforward. One offers the animal a choice between two alternatives, such as two places or two activities, and then observes the relative frequency with which it chooses each. Considering the data on learning a new behavior, one is immediately inclined to test, by a choice procedure, for the relative attractiveness of a goal box that was rewarded 100 per cent of the time and a goal box that was partially rewarded. Fortunately, such studies are available in the literature. And, unfortunately, the results of these studies seem, at first glance, to be at variance with our theoretical expectations.

D'Amato, Lachman, and Kivy (1958) report a study in which they tested the relative attractiveness of one goal box that had been associated with continuous reward and another that had been associated with partial reward. A *single* group of animals was taught to run an alley. On some trials this led to a goal box that always contained food; on the remainder of the trials, it led to a distinctively different goal box that contained food on only 50 per cent of the trials. Following this training, all animals were given 30 free choice trials on a single unit T-maze with the two goal boxes, both empty, at opposite arms of the maze. The results show that during the first 15 trials the animals made significantly more choices of the 100 per cent rewarded box than of the 50 per cent rewarded one. This preference was quite consistent. Afterward, from the sixteenth trial on, there was no clear preference for either of the two boxes. In fact, the animals became reluctant to choose. This same finding of an initial preference for a goal box that had been continuously rewarded over one that had been partially rewarded is also reported by Mason (1957), using a more complex training procedure. How can one explain the apparent contradiction between these data and our interpretation of the results of the "learning a new task" experiment? There we came to the conclusion that partial reward, combining the effects of dissonance reduction and secondary reward, resulted in stronger attractions than secondary reward alone. Here we find data that tend to indicate the opposite.

Let us, however, look more closely at the procedure of these experiments in relation to the details of the dissonance formulation. It must be remembered that in the choice experiments mentioned above, the animal is choosing between alternatives on which it has had different experiences concerning food. Thus, one must clearly distinguish the early stages of the choice trials from later stages. At first, when faced with the choice, the animal's behavior is guided largely by its expectations concerning the availability of food. Certainly it is not inconsistent with dissonance theory (or any other theory) for the animal to prefer a place where it expects food on every trial to one where it expects only occasional reward. The extra attractions developed through dissonance reduction can hardly be expected to overcome this difference. It is only in later choice trials, when the animal no longer expects differential reward between the two goal boxes, that the choices would be sensitive to the extra attractions that may have developed.

There remains one disturbing aspect about these data. It

will be recalled that in the D'Amato, Lachman, and Kivy experiment, there was no preference for either goal box in the last 15 trials. By this time, however, food expectations should have been much reduced and the choice behavior should have reflected whatever extra attractions existed. Why, then, did not the animals prefer the partially rewarded to the continuously rewarded box during these later choice trials? Our explanation hinges around the conditions necessary for the development and maintenance of extra attractions. As we have emphasized, these accumulate only in circumstances where the animal does not change its behavior. If, after this accumulation of attractiveness through dissonance reduction has started, the animal is induced to change its behavior, these extra attractions weaken. In the free choice situation of the present experiment the conditions are so arranged that, during the initial trials, the animal is induced to go consistently to the 100 per cent goal box and to avoid the partially rewarded one. This should lead to at least a partial breakdown of the attractions that had been established in the latter during training, and by the time expectation of food has vanished as a factor, there should be little basis for a choice of either box.

In summary, it is clear that this type of experiment does not give any direct support to our interpretation. But at least the results are not contradictory with our formulation. We would expect the initial preference for the continuously rewarded goal box. Our explanation of why the animals do not eventually show a preference for the partially rewarded one, though plausible, may seem weak and *post hoc*, but it has implications that can be tested. If it is correct, we should be able to set up choice situations where the animal is not induced consistently to avoid the partially rewarded goal box during the initial test trials. Under these circumstances we should expect the extra attractions to show themselves clearly once the effects of food expectation had worn off. Fortunately, there are such experimental arrangements reported in the literature.

D'Amato, Lachman, and Kivy (1958), in the same article referred to previously, report a second experiment in which *two* groups of animals were trained on a runway. One group received reward 100 per cent of the time, the other only 50 per cent of the time. Both groups were then tested for 30 trials in a free choice situation. Now, however, the goal box of the runway was at the end of one arm of the T-maze and the start box of the runway was at the end of the other arm. The assumption was that the start box was a familiar but relatively neutral place.

During the first 15 free choice trials both the 100 per cent and the 50 per cent groups showed a decided preference for the previously rewarded goal box over the start box. As one might expect, if dissonance reduction was not complete by the end of training, there was a tendency for the 100 per cent group to choose the goal box somewhat more frequently during the initial trials than did the 50 per cent group. The important thing, however, is that the partially rewarded animals did go to the goal box; they were not induced to avoid it. Our expectation, therefore, is that the extra attractions for these animals that were established through dissonance reduction should not have weakened and their effects should be apparent on later trials. This is borne out in the last 15 test trials. Here we find that the animals in the 100 per cent rewarded group showed a decline in the frequency with which they chose the goal box, whereas the 50 per cent rewarded animals continued to choose it very consistently. Thus, as long as the animal is not led to change its behavior during the initial testing trials, there is evidence that partial reward establishes stronger attractions than does continuous reward. Exactly the same kind of results have been reported by Klein (1959) and by Saltzman (1949). Thus, there is evidence from both new learning and preference tests that dissonance-producing experiences do lead to the development of extra attractions that are at least as strong, and possibly stronger, than those produced by secondary reward.

### Persistence During Extinction

A measure of resistance to extinction would seem to be one of the most obvious ways of testing for any extra attractions that have developed in a situation, and if we can assume that even a weak attraction tends to prolong extinction, such a test should prove highly sensitive. Unlike a new learning procedure, it would not involve changes in activity and environment between training and testing, nor would it involve the problems connected with choices between alternatives which we discussed earlier. In extinction, even weak attractions would have a good chance of showing their effects by increasing persistence in the task. This is precisely the logic that has led to the use of extinction tests in demonstrating secondary reward effects.

However, inferences from an extinction test for the present purposes present some difficulties that are not encountered using tests based on new learning or preference behavior. One is quite willing to admit that, if an animal learns a new task in order to get to an empty goal box, there are sources of attraction in that box. Similarly one is willing to accept that, if an animal chooses alternative A over alternative B, the former has attractions not found in the latter. If, however, we point to the data which show that partial reward, delay of reward, and effort greatly prolong extinction, many would be less willing to regard them as supporting the idea that special attractions have developed. Throughout its history learning theory has appealed to very different factors in attempting to explain increased resistance to extinction. Because it is concerned with explaining the strengthening and weakening of associations between stimuli and responses, learning theory has emphasized factors such as stimulus similarities between training and extinction trials, adaptation effects, and changes in the drive level of the animal. With theoretical thinking channeled in these directions, the possibility that differences in extinction rates may actually be a measurement of relative degrees of attractiveness in a situation has been largely ignored. Therefore, if we wish to argue in favor of this notion, it is necessary that we show at least two things: (1) that known attractions, even if weak, can prolong extinction in a manner similar to that observed when a partial reward group is contrasted with a continuously rewarded one; and (2) that when an animal has dissonance-producing experiences in an end-box, the box will act like a known attraction when it is present during extinction trials. If these two things can be shown, we may then convincingly interpret many of the differences observed in extinction rates as a measurement of relative attractiveness.

In order to test the first proposition, that known, weak attractions will prolong extinction, we made use of the fact that the white rat seemingly prefers dark places to bright ones. In the following experiment this was tested using a brightness differential chosen to produce only a weak difference in attractiveness.

*Experiment 2.—Influence of Natural Attractions on Extinction*

The basic idea of this experiment was to train two groups of animals in a comparable fashion, both with 100 per cent reward, but with a slightly more attractive goal box for one group than for the other. To obtain this differential attractiveness, we used a brightness difference, since, as we have mentioned earlier, there is considerable evidence that rats have a preference for the darker of two otherwise identical places.

To be sure that this preference existed in our animals, and to be sure that we were dealing with only a small difference in attractiveness, we first set up the following test situation. Two identical goal boxes were constructed, the rear walls consisting of milk-glass plates. A 100-watt lamp could be placed behind either of them and, when lighted, would diffuse the goal box with a medium degree of brightness. One of these boxes was placed at each end of the arm in a T-maze.

Eight hungry rats, after being tamed and adapted to the apparatus, were given preference runs in this situation. They were released in the stem of the T and then permitted to make a choice between the two boxes. On half of the trials the right goal box was lighted and the left was dark; on the other half the left box was lighted and the right was dark. Both boxes contained food on each trial.

In this situation the animals failed to show any preference between the two boxes. Instead they immediately settled into position habits, always running either to the right or left side, regardless of whether that box was lighted or not. Clearly, any difference in attractiveness between the lighted and unlighted boxes was too weak to reveal itself on this test.

The apparatus was then rearranged so that the entrances to both goal boxes were side by side and faced directly toward the starting box. This latter box had a clear glass gate which enabled the animal, during a 10-second restraining period, to see the interior of each goal box. Again, each of these boxes contained food on every trial, with the left box being lighted on half of the trials and the right one on the remainder. A second group of eight hungry animals was given preference tests in this new situation. After the 10-second restraining period, the glass door of the start box was raised and the animal was permitted to make a choice. Each animal was given 16 spaced trials.

Under these conditions, the animals did show a definite preference for the dark compartment. Eighty-three per cent of all choices were for the dark side even though this varied from right to left in a random manner. It should be noted that seven of the eight animals made one or more runs to the lighted side, but all of the animals chose the darker side in a majority of the trials. One can conclude that there was a preference for the darker compartment. This preference seemed rather weak, however, showing up only under special test conditions.

Having established that a relatively weak differential attraction existed, we then measured its influence on extinction behavior. Two new groups of animals were tamed and placed on a 22-hour hunger cycle. One group of nine animals was trained to run a 6-foot alley with a lighted goal box at the end of it on each trial. They were given 36 spaced runs over a 9-day period. Each run was rewarded with a pellet of food. A second group of eight animals was trained in exactly the same way, but with a dark goal box. All animals were then given 36 spaced extinction trials. If during extinction an animal had not entered the goal box within 60 seconds from the time the start box door was raised, it was removed from the apparatus.

The running times for the two groups during training were indistinguishable. There was no evidence that the group running to the lighted box had any hesitancy about entering. During extinction, however, the two groups tended to diverge, as shown in Figure 3.2. The animals running to the dark box tended to run faster than those going to the lighted box. By the third day of extinction the average running times for the two groups differed, the difference being significant between

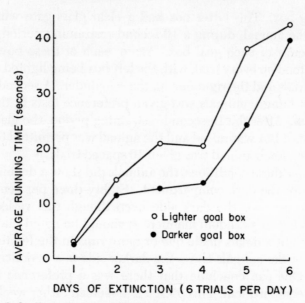

FIG. 3.2.—RESISTANCE TO EXTINCTION AS AFFECTED BY THE BRIGHT-
NESS OF THE GOAL BOX (EXPERIMENT 2)

the .05 and .02 levels of significance. Using a *post hoc* extinction criterion of four 30-second trials, not necessarily consecutive, the median number of trials to reach this criterion is 23
for the light group and 30 for the dark group. This difference
is significant between the .05 and .10 levels. Thus, although
the differences are not huge and dramatic, they are nonetheless
in the direction expected, considering that the animals have a
slight preference for the dark box. It should be recalled that the
preference for the darker of the two boxes was very weak. Thus,
we may conclude that slight attractions of this sort have an
effect on extinction data even when the attraction is unrelated
to the dominant motivation.

We have shown that weak, natural attractions do prolong
extinction. The next step is to show that dissonance-producing
experiences have a comparable effect when associations between the running response and the training-task stimuli are
not crucial, that is, when past experience with the goal box is
the only relevant variable. We could do this by comparing two
groups which, during extinction, both run an alley associated

with 100 per cent reward. One group, however, runs to a goal box in which it has experienced partial reward while the other group runs to a goal box in which it has always been rewarded.

Since we could find no experiments in the literature that satisfied this requirement, we conducted our own. Our experiment was designed to answer the question of whether or not goal box attractions were independent of the schedules of reward associated with the task used during extinction.

## Experiment 3.—*Runway vs. Goal Box Effects*

Two very distinctive runways and two very distinctive goal boxes were used in this study. The goal boxes were interchangeable with each of the runways so as to form four different task and goal box combinations. Each animal was given trials on each of these combinations in a random order. On three of the combinations the animal was rewarded on each run. On the remaining combination the plan was never to reward the animal. This design would mean that one goal box and one runway would be associated with 100 per cent reward, and the other goal box and the other runway would be associated with 50 per cent reward.

In this design all animals have exactly the same history of training. Consequently, if some of the animals are extinguished on the 100 per cent runway, half with the 100 per cent goal box present and half with the 50 per cent goal box, any differences in persistence must be attributed to the past experiences with the specific goal boxes. Similarly, if the rest of the animals are extinguished on the 50 per cent runway, half with each goal box, any difference in persistence between these two must also be attributed to the goal boxes. Thus, we have two tests of our hypothesis that experiences of dissonance and dissonance reduction associated with a goal box can prolong extinction independently of the animal's prior experiences on the task. Table 3.2 summarizes the design of the experiment.

The 24 rats used in this study were tamed, placed on a 22-hour food-deprivation schedule for several days, and then adapted to eating food pellets in the two goal boxes. They were then given 3 rewarded trials on each of the runway–goal box combinations. Thereafter, they were given 8 trials a day, at 15-minute

TABLE 3.2

DESIGN OF PRELIMINARY EXPERIMENT ON RUNWAY VS.
GOAL BOX EFFECTS (EXPERIMENT 3)

| | History of Reward on | |
| --- | --- | --- |
| | Extinction Runway | Extinction Goal Box |
| Group 1 | 100% | 50% |
| Group 2 | 100% | 100% |
| Group 3 | 50% | 50% |
| Group 4 | 50% | 100% |

Note: All animals had identical training experience with all four possible combinations of runway and goal box.

intervals, for the next 20 days. All animals ran each of the four combinations of runway and goal box equally often but in an unpredictable order.

It was found partway through this training that a few of the animals were beginning to make a discrimination. They became hesitant to enter the 50 per cent goal box when it was paired with the 50 per cent runway (the combination that was never rewarded), but they would enter it readily when it was paired with the 100 per cent runway. To counteract this tendency, during the last 14 training trials on the 50 per cent runway–50 per cent goal box combination, 6 of the runs were rewarded in an unpredictable manner. As a result of these 6 rewarded trials the 50 per cent runway and the 50 per cent goal box were actually rewarded 57.5 per cent of the time.

At the completion of training, the animals were divided into four groups of six each. One of these groups was extinguished on each of the four combinations of runway and goal box. Running times, from the raising of the start box door until entrance into the goal box, were taken on each trial both during training and extinction. Extinction trials were given at the rate of 8 a day, with at least 15 minutes between trials. The criterion of extinction was 6 trials, not necessarily consecutive, on which an animal failed to enter the goal box within 120 seconds. On such trials it was removed directly from the apparatus. On all other trials it was retained in the goal box for 20 seconds before being removed.

By the third day of extinction, the differences among the groups were clear and definite. Table 3.3 presents the average

TABLE 3.3

AVERAGE RUNNING TIMES (IN SECONDS) ON THIRD
DAY OF EXTINCTION (EXPERIMENT 3)

| Runway | Goal Box | |
|---|---|---|
| | 100% | Partial |
| 100% | 67.9 | 28.1 |
| Partial | 48.0 | 23.2 |

running times for each group of animals on the third day of extinction. This day was chosen rather than a later one since, on subsequent days, many animals were discontinued because they had reached the criterion of extinction.

It is clear from the table that partial reward has an effect on prolonging running during extinction both when the partial reward is associated with the runway and when it is associated with the goal box. The difference in running times between the 100 per cent and the partially rewarded goal box groups is significant at better than the .05 level. The difference between the runway conditions, although favoring the partially rewarded runway, is not significant. Precisely the same pattern of results is shown by the number of trials to the criterion of extinction as indicated in Table 3.4. Again, the partially rewarded goal box makes for a big increase in resistance to extinction, significant beyond the .05 level. The partially rewarded runway makes for a smaller difference which is not statistically significant. Obviously, even if runway stimuli are associated with 100 per cent reward, partial reward experiences in the goal box have a marked effect on resistance to extinction. Indeed, it would appear that dissonance-reducing experiences in a goal box have resulted in the development of extra attractions. From the point of view of dissonance theory, since attractions can also be expected to develop in connection with the activity, it is not surprising to find that the runway experiences also have some effect.

TABLE 3.4

GEOMETRIC MEAN OF TRIALS TO EXTINCTION
(EXPERIMENT 3)

| Runway | Goal Box | |
|---|---|---|
| | 100% | Partial |
| 100% | 38.9 | 55.0 |
| Partial | 47.9 | 75.9 |

There are, of course, a number of difficulties with these data. First of all, there were relatively few animals; second, there was the difficulty during training that has been mentioned; and finally, we did not counterbalance for initial preferences of specific runway or goal box. For these reasons a second and more elaborate study was designed to avoid these difficulties.

## Experiment 4.—A Replication of Runway vs. Goal Box Effects

In this study, 60 rats, half of them males and half females, were used. After taming, establishment of a 22-hour hunger cycle, and adaptation to the goal boxes, they were divided into five groups of 12 animals, with an equal number of males and females in each. Four of these were experimental groups and the fifth was a control. The same two runways and goal boxes were used as in the previous experiment. One runway, painted gray, had four right-angle turns in the sequence left, right, right, left. Each of the four sections was 17 inches long. Four hurdles, each 4 inches high, were spaced at equal distances throughout the runway. The second runway was a straight alley, 48 inches long, which contained four wooden doors under which the animal had to push. This runway also was painted gray. The same starting box was used for both runways. One of the goal boxes was 13 inches long, 9 inches wide, and 7 inches high. The floor was of wood and the interior was painted black. The entrance to it was at one end so that, after the animal entered, it ran straight forward to the food dish. The second goal box was 18 inches long, 7 inches wide, and 7 inches high. The walls were of unpainted plywood and the floor was hardware cloth. The entrance was on one side so that, after the animal entered, it had to turn to the right in order to reach the food cup. Both boxes had guillotine entrance doors.

The design of the study, similar to the previous one, can be illustrated by considering one experimental group. This group was given 8 trials a day with at least half an hour between trials. In a day's run, each of the four combinations of runway and goal box occurred twice, but not in any set order. On three of these combinations, the animal was rewarded with a wet mash pellet on each run. On the fourth combination, it was rewarded only 25 per cent of the time, in an unpredictable sequence. It is apparent from this description that one runway and one goal box were associated with 100 per cent reward while the others were associated with 62.5 per cent reward. Any pre-experimental preferences for a specific goal box or runway were counterbalanced by having the partial reward associated with a different combination for each of the four experimental groups. The fifth, or control group, was run in exactly the same way as an experimental group except that all combinations were rewarded 100 per cent of the time. All animals were run for 24 days, which resulted in 36 unrewarded runs for the experimental animals. On unrewarded trials, the animal was left in the goal box for 20 seconds.

At the completion of training, each group was divided into four subgroups of three animals each. One of these was extinguished on each of the four combinations of runway and goal box. Thus, for the experimental groups, one subgroup was extinguished on a combination involving a partially rewarded runway and a partially rewarded goal box, a second on a partially rewarded runway and a 100 per cent rewarded goal box, a third on a runway rewarded 100 per cent of the time with a partially rewarded goal box, and the fourth on a runway and goal box each of which had been rewarded 100 per cent of the time. Extinction trials were given at the rate of six a day, with at least 30 minutes between trials. The criterion of extinction was five trials, not necessarily consecutive, on which the animal refused to enter the goal box within 120 seconds. On these trials the animal was removed from the apparatus. On trials when the animal did enter the goal box, it was kept there 20 seconds before being removed.

The 12 animals in the control group showed no significant differences in speed of running on each of the four combinations of runway and goal box on the last four days of training (average of 5.5 seconds). There are no apparent differences among the four combinations in terms of difficulty or preference. A similar analysis for the four experimental groups also shows no significant differences among the four training combinations or among the four training groups. However, when the data were grouped according to whether or not a runway–goal box combination was associated with partial reward, there were differ-

TABLE 3.5

AVERAGE RUNNING TIMES (IN SECONDS) DURING LAST FOUR
DAYS OF TRAINING (EXPERIMENT 4)

| Runway | Goal Box | |
| --- | --- | --- |
| | 100% | Partial |
| 100% | 4.7 | 4.6 |
| Partial | 5.3 | 6.3 |

ences significant between the .01 and .05 levels. Table 3.5
shows these data. There is some tendency for the animals to
run more slowly on a runway associated with partial reward
than on one associated with 100 per cent reward. On the other
hand, whether or not the goal box has been associated with partial reward has no measurable effect on running speed during
training. This lack of difference is undoubtedly due to the fact
that the animal did not know which box was present until it
arrived there.

The results for the average running time on the third day
of extinction, and for the average number of trials to the extinction criterion, are presented in Tables 3.6 and 3.7, respectively. It can be seen that the same pattern of results is obtained here as in the previous study. Animals running to a
partially rewarded goal box extinguish at a considerably slower
rate than animals running to a continuously rewarded one. This
difference is significant only at the .15 level for running times
on the third day, but it is significant at the .01 level for trials
to extinction. Partial reward on the runway has a similar effect
on both measures, but neither of these differences is statistically
significant.

It will be recalled that in this experiment there was a control group that never experienced partial reward during train-

TABLE 3.6

AVERAGE RUNNING TIMES (IN SECONDS) ON THIRD DAY OF
EXTINCTION (EXPERIMENT 4)

| Runway | Goal Box | |
| --- | --- | --- |
| | 100% | Partial |
| 100% | 34.8 | 24.3 |
| Partial | 32.9 | 21.8 |

TABLE 3.7
GEOMETRIC MEAN OF TRIALS TO EXTINCTION
(EXPERIMENT 4)

| Runway | Goal Box | |
|--------|------|---------|
| | 100% | Partial |
| 100% | 29.4 | 37.2 |
| Partial | 30.7 | 44.3 |

ing. The results for this control group are interesting. The average running time for these animals on the third day of extinction was 87.8 seconds, significantly slower (.01 level) than any of the other groups. They also reached the criterion of extinction in an average of 19.4 trials, which is also significantly less (.01 level) than any of the other groups. A comparison of these figures with the comparable ones for the experimental group, which was extinguished on a combination of runway and goal box that had always been 100 per cent rewarded, raises some problems. For all four experimental groups, the generalized effect of partial rewards must be rather great: this is the only conceivable explanation of the difference between two groups that, during extinction, are both running in a situation that was always associated with 100 per cent reward. Such a degree of generalization in this particular experimental situation should occasion no surprise in the reader, in view of the similarities between goal boxes and runways and the ever changing situations in which each animal was trained.

Such generalization effects also may have considerably reduced the magnitudes of the differences we observed among our experimental groups. Any generalization from runway to runway and from goal box to goal box would have weakened the obtained differences. But, for the point we set out to make, this is unimportant. We have demonstrated that, as the result of partial reward, there is an effect specific to the goal box which results in increased resistance to extinction. This finding makes it plausible to infer the existence of some extra attraction which has developed through dissonance reduction.

Let us, then, summarize where we stand. We have shown that, if we add a weak food incentive to a new learning situation, animals that have been partially rewarded in the goal box

82     THE DEVELOPMENT OF ATTRACTIONS

will learn the new task more quickly in order to reach that goal
box than will animals that have been continuously rewarded
there.  In addition, existing literature reveals that preference
for a partially rewarded place over a continuously rewarded
one can be demonstrated as long as the conditions of the test
do not induce the animal to go away from the partially rewarded
place initially in its search for food.

We have also shown that if a known weak preference exists
for one goal box over another, animals trained to the preferred
box extinguish more slowly than do animals trained to the less
preferred one.  The existing literature shows that partial reward
tends to prolong extinction in a comparable fashion.  From these
two findings, it is clear that the partial reward results could be
due to the development of extra attractions.  Finally, we have
reported an experiment demonstrating that partial reward experience with a specific goal box prolongs resistance to extinction regardless of whether or not the runway has been associated with partial reward.  All of these findings are directly
implied by a dissonance reduction interpretation which postu-
lates the development of extra attractions.

Let us look at the relevance of these data to the alternative
explanations that we discussed in Chapter 1.  Many of those explanations, particularly those of Weinstock and Amsel, emphasize that partial reward experiences ultimately produce associations between stimuli specific to the runway and the running
response.  Amsel, for example, assumes that runway stimuli
eventually arouse anticipatory frustration responses which
finally become conditioned to running to the goal box.  Such
an explanation seems to imply that if, after partial reward training, changes are made in the runway or in the activity required,
the partial reward effect might largely disappear.

If, however, one accepts the data we have presented about
the learning of a new task, preference tests in a T-maze, and
the results of our experiments on runway versus goal box effects,
doubt is cast on the validity of such alternative explanations.
Clearly, even though the task the animal must do to get to the
goal box is drastically changed, partial reward effects can still
be observed.  Our own experiments have shown that runways

associated with 100 per cent reward scarcely reduce the effect on extinction of the presence of a goal box associated with partial reward.

To what degree do the data we have presented in this chapter force us to accept the interpretation that partial reward leads to the development of extra attractions? The data we have discussed on new learning, choice behavior, and specificity of goal box effects make a reasonably strong case for such extra attractions. Other theorists, however, might question whether or not an explanation in terms of "adaptation" for unpleasantness or frustration is not equally forceful. To the extent that this alternative is merely a verbal preference, it need not concern us. We readily grant that unrewarded trials are unpleasant for an animal expecting food. Our interpretation also grants that, eventually, the animal finds such situations less unpleasant because of the extra attractions it has discovered. In the situations with which we deal, the rat never completely reduces dissonance, and unrewarded trials undoubtedly continue to be unpleasant to some degree.

What else may be meant by "adaptation" to unpleasantness or frustration? The real issue is the specific mechanism that is proposed theoretically to underly "adaptation" effects. Later in the book, particularly in connection with minimal motivation experiments reported in Chapter 6 and with experiments on effort reported in Chapter 7, we shall support the interpretation that dissonance reduction leading to extra attractions is, indeed, the mechanism which operates.

All of the data we have discussed in this chapter have been concerned with the effects of partial reward. It would be desirable to have comparable data showing that delay of reward and effort expenditure lead to the same effects. Unfortunately, data from which attraction may be inferred do not exist in the literature. Indeed, it would not be easy to collect such data in an unambiguous way for situations involving choice and for the learning of new tasks when the effort variable is involved. It is much easier to study the effects of effort and delay of reward using the extinction procedure. In the next several chapters, we shall present evidence of this sort.

# 4

# Cumulative Effects of Dissonance Reduction

In the previous chapter, we presented evidence that extra attractions do result from dissonance reduction. The development of these attractions, according to the theory, occurs in the following way. The animal performs an action and then finds that the consequences of this act do not justify it, that is, little or no extrinsic reward is present. This results in a motivational state, dissonance, which tends to reduce or resolve itself. As long as the animal does not change its course of action, the major way in which this dissonance reduction can occur is through the discovery of aspects of the situation that satisfy some of its subordinate motives, thus providing at least partial justification for the action undertaken. Nevertheless, as long as these extra attractions provide only partial rather than complete justification, dissonance is again aroused on the next similar occasion. This, in turn, leads to further attempts at dissonance reduction and thus to the gradual accumulation of extra attractions.

Phrased in this way, it is clear that two things are implied about the effects of dissonance reduction: first, the discovery of these extra attractions tends to occur primarily on the dissonance-producing trial; and second, the strength of these extra attractions is an increasing function of the number of such dissonance-producing experiences. In this chapter, we shall be concerned with experimental evidence pertaining to these implications in partial reward training.

Our theory, then, asserts that the strength of extra attractions is a cumulative function of the number of dissonance-producing experiences. However, the usual empirical statement is that resistance to extinction varies inversely with the *percentage* of rewarded trials. Animals rewarded 75 per cent of the time extinguish more rapidly than those rewarded 50 per cent of the time, and the latter extinguish more rapidly than those rewarded 25 per cent of the time. This implies that it is the ratio of rewarded to unrewarded trials that is the important variable. This statement of the relationship is consistent with Humphreys' hypothesis (1939), but is clearly at variance with ours.

Is this, however, a correct statement of the empirical relation that exists? We must keep in mind that the statement is based on experimental studies that, uniformally, have contrasted various reward schedules in which either the total number of trials or the number of rewarded trials have been equated for the various groups. Such procedures make it impossible to assert whether the percentage of rewarded trials or the number of unrewarded trials is the important variable since the two are confounded in the design. For instance, suppose we compare three groups of animals, one with 75 per cent, a second with 50 per cent, and a third with 25 per cent reward, each group having received a total of 60 training trials. The first group, as a consequence, has only 15 unrewarded trials, the second 30, and the third 45. With this perfect negative correlation between percentage of reward and the number of unrewarded trials, we are of course unable to decide which of the variables is the crucial one in determining resistance to extinction.

A decision based on experimental data is important for our theory and also for any form of discrimination theory that depends for its explanation on contrast between training and extinction conditions.

*Experimental Data on Cumulative Effects*

Two studies in the literature are pertinent to this issue and, at the same time, suggest the correct experimental design for making a critical test. One of these (Lewis and Cotton, 1959) compares 50 per cent reward groups that received either 16 or 60 training trials. They observe that the rats that received more training trials take longer to extinguish; but since they failed to include any 100 per cent reward groups in their experiment they did not seem to appreciate the importance of their result. The same result is reported in a study by M. G. Weinstock (1957). She was primarily interested in studying the effect of the time spent in the goal box on unrewarded trials on resistance to extinction after partial reward. This did not prove to be a significant variable. As part of her design, however, she varied the number of training trials for some partial reward groups while keeping the percentage of reward constant. Consequently, from her data we can determine whether or not resistance to extinction increases as a function of the number of unrewarded trials.

Specifically, she ran a continuously rewarded and a 50 per cent rewarded group on a runway. Half of each group received 30 training trials and the other half received 60. Trials were spaced 15 minutes apart. All animals were given 30 extinction trials with the same spacing. Half of the animals were confined in the goal box for 10 seconds during extinction; the other half for 30 seconds. The average running speeds for the last 15 extinction trials are shown in Table 4.1.

It is apparent that the additional training trials had little effect on resistance to extinction for the 100 per cent groups, but a very considerable one for the partially rewarded animals. The interaction between the number of training trials and the schedule of reward was significant beyond the .01 level regardless of time spent in the goal box. Clearly, resistance to extinction appears to increase directly with the number of unrewarded trials.

TABLE 4.1

AVERAGE RUNNING SPEEDS DURING EXTINCTION AFTER DIFFERENT NUMBERS OF TRAINING TRIALS*

| Time in Goal Box | Percentage of Reward | Number of Training Trials | |
|---|---|---|---|
| | | 30 | 60 |
| 10 seconds | 100% | 20 | 17 |
| 10 seconds | 50% | 22 | 34 |
| 30 seconds | 100% | 12 | 15 |
| 30 seconds | 50% | 15 | 34 |

* Data from Weinstock (1957).

Although these results support our dissonance formulation, which emphasizes the unrewarded trial as the important factor, they are open to criticism from adherents of other hypotheses. It can be argued that thirty trials are not sufficient to acquaint an animal with the relative frequency of reward involved. Furthermore, since only one percentage of partial reward was used, it is impossible to determine whether or not the variable of percentage of reward has an effect over and above that which can be attributed to the number of unrewarded trials. Weinstock's study does, however, suggest the proper design for contrasting the effects of the number of unrewarded trials with the effects of the percentage of rewards. What is required are several groups of animals, some on different partial reward schedules but equated for the number of unrewarded trials involved, others on the same partial reward schedule but varying in the number of unrewarded trials. Under these conditions, the two variables can be separately evaluated. Such a study not being available in the literature, we designed and carried out our own.

*Experiment 5.—The Cumulative Effect of Unrewarded Trials*

A total of 146 white rats were used in the experiment. They were approximately ninety days old at the start of training. Six of these were discarded before extinction began either because of illness or death. All animals were tamed and then placed on a deprivation schedule during which they had free access to food for two hours each day. This schedule was maintained throughout the experiment so that the animals had been without food for about twenty hours at the beginning of each day's run.

The apparatus was an S-shaped runway. The first 9-inch section was the start box and the last 17-inch section was the goal box. The latter contained a food cup with a tube leading into it. Food could be dropped through this tube on rewarded trials once the animal had entered the goal box. Spaced at approximately equal intervals throughout the runway were three plywood swinging doors. These were set at a 60-degree angle with respect to the floor so that the animals could push under them. At each of the two turns of the runway there was a 3-inch-high hurdle for the animal to climb over. The start box and runway were unpainted, but the goal compartment was black. The whole apparatus was 6 inches deep and was covered with hardware cloth.

The apparatus and procedure differed from the usual partial reward study in minor ways. The activity required of the animal involved a far greater expenditure of effort than is common. We made this requirement because, on theoretical grounds, the magnitude of the dissonance produced on an unrewarded trial should be a function of at least two things: (1) the failure of the animal to find food when it expected and was oriented toward food; and (2) the amount of effort the animal expended to get to the place where it expected to find food. Thus, if the theory is correct, a very effortful task should enhance the effect of dissonance reduction. However, the use of this very effortful activity required that all animals have a long period of preliminary training before the partial reward schedules could be introduced; otherwise, many of them would have refused to perform.

Preliminary training consisted of first adapting the animal to eating wet mash pellets in the goal box. It was then given 2 rewarded runs through the apparatus with all the doors open and the hurdles removed. During the next 17 days, the animal was given a total of 84 rewarded trials, during which the doors were gradually lowered and the hurdles increased to full height. For 4 following days, it was given 6 rewarded trials each day with full effort expenditure required. Thus, there was a total of 112 preliminary trials, with constant apparatus conditions during the last 24. All of these trials, as well as the subsequent training and extinction ones, were spaced at least 15 minutes apart.

Eleven different groups of animals, roughly matched on the basis of running times during the last 4 days of preliminary training, were used in this experiment. There were 11 to 16 animals in each group, approximately half males and half females. Because of the large number of animals involved, and the large number of trials required in some conditions, not all groups of rats were started at the same time. Altogether, the data collection lasted almost one calendar year.

Partial reward schedules were introduced on the day following the completion of preliminary training. Thereafter, animals were given 6 training trials a day. On rewarded trials the ani-

mal was given a large wet mash pellet which took an average
of 40 seconds to eat; on unrewarded trials the animal was kept
in the goal compartment for the same length of time.

The over-all design of the experiment, that is, the exact number of unrewarded trials and the total number of trials given to
animals in each of the eleven experimental conditions, is shown
in Table 4.2. It can be seen that three different groups of animals were run with a 33 per cent reward schedule. The total
number of trials they received was varied so that one group experienced 16 unrewarded trials, a second group experienced 27
unrewarded trials, and a third group experienced 72 unrewarded
trials. Similarly, three different groups were run on a 50 per
cent reward schedule, each group experiencing either 16, 27, or
72 unrewarded trials. To save experimental time, only two
groups were run on a 67 per cent reward schedule. The group
that would have experienced 27 unrewarded trials was omitted.

It is clear from an examination of the table that the total
number of training trials varies considerably. The smallest number of trials after preliminary training is 24 for the 33 per cent
reward group that experienced 16 unrewarded trials. The largest number of total trials following preliminary training is 216
for the group that experienced 72 unrewarded trials on a 67 per
cent reward schedule. In order to have a comparison for the

TABLE 4.2

TOTAL NUMBER OF TRIALS BEYOND PRELIMINARY TRAINING FOR
EACH GROUP IN PARTIAL REWARD EXPERIMENT (EXPERIMENT 5)

| Reward Schedule | Number of Unrewarded Trials | | | |
|---|---|---|---|---|
| | 0 | 16 | 27 | 72 |
| 33% | | 24 (14)* | 42 (11) | 108 (16) |
| 50% | | 31† (12) | 54 (13) | 144 (13) |
| 67% | | 48 (11) | — — | 216 (11) |
| 100% | 0 (11) 54 (14) 216 (14) | | | |

* Numbers in parentheses refer to the number of animals in each group.
† One extra unrewarded trial was given to the animals in this group to bring the number of unrewarded trials to 16 in 5 days of partial reward training.

effect of sheer total number of trials, three different groups were run with 100 per cent reward. One of these groups began extinction immediately after the preliminary training was finished. No additional trials were given. A second group was given 54 trials, and a third group was given 216 additional trials before extinction was started. Thus, the range of total number of trials for the three groups on a 100 per cent reward schedule brackets closely the range of total number of trials of the partially rewarded animals.

During training, the order of rewarded and unrewarded trials was prearranged so as to be unsystematic within each day. However, of the 6 trials each day there were 4 unrewarded trials in the 33 per cent group, 3 in the 50 per cent group, and 2 in the 67 per cent group. The last trial on the last day before extinction was rewarded for all animals in all conditions. Extinction trials were run in the same manner as the acquisition trials—that is, each animal was given 6 trials a day, spaced at intervals of at least 15 minutes. Of course, no food was obtained in the food compartment on extinction trials. When the animal entered the food compartment it was kept there for 40 seconds and then returned to its home cage. If the animal did not enter the food compartment within 180 seconds after the start box door was raised, it was taken out of the apparatus. Six such trials, not necessarily consecutive, were used as a criterion of extinction.

The main over-all results of this experiment are presented in Table 4.3 and in Figure 4.1. These present the average num-

TABLE 4.3

AVERAGE NUMBER OF TRIALS TO
EXTINCTION—GEOMETRIC MEANS (EXPERIMENT 5)

| Reward Schedule | Number of Unrewarded Trials | | | |
|---|---|---|---|---|
| | 0 | 16 | 27 | 72 |
| 33% | | 26.3 | 32.3 | 54.5 |
| 50% | | 26.7 | 36.1 | 47.3 |
| 67% | | 30.2 | — | 55.5 |
| 100% (zero trials) | 15.2 | | | |
| 100% (54 trials) | 19.8 | | | |
| 100% (216 trials) | 22.5 | | | |

ber of trials required by each of the eleven groups to reach the criterion of extinction. The data are presented, and were analyzed, in terms of geometric means for two reasons. First of all, the distributions of number of trials to reach the criterion are highly skewed. Using logarithms tends to normalize them and to facilitate statistical analysis. The other reason is apparent in Figure 4.1. Presenting the data in these terms makes the relationships pleasingly linear.

The results for the groups rewarded 100 per cent of the time show the influence on extinction of the number of training trials involved. It is clear from Table 4.3 that all three of these groups extinguish very quickly. The geometric means are 15.2, 19.8, and 22.5 trials, respectively, for the groups having 0, 54, and 216 trials in addition to preliminary training. To realize fully how rapid this extinction is, one must remember that these means include the 6 criterion trials on which the animals refused

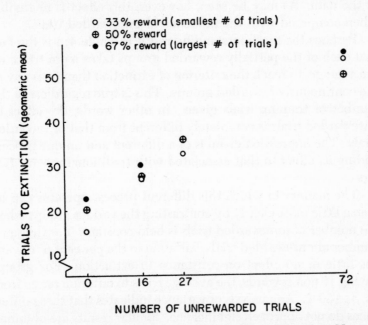

FIG. 4.1.—RESISTANCE TO EXTINCTION AS A FUNCTION OF THE NUMBER OF UNREWARDED TRIALS (EXPERIMENT 5). N.B. For those groups receiving zero unrewarded trials (100 per cent reward) the filled circle represents the largest number of trials and the open circle, the smallest number.

to enter the goal compartment within 180 seconds. Increasing the number of trials for continuously rewarded groups obviously has some effect on resistance to extinction. This effect, however, is slight. An analysis of variance indicates that the difference among these three groups is significant at the .05 level, but most of this difference is due to the very rapid extinction of the group that had zero additional trials after preliminary training. The difference between the 54 and 216 trial groups is small and not significant. Undoubtedly, the zero trial group had not adjusted adequately to the effortful task by the end of preliminary training. This is reflected in the running times of the three groups on the last day of training: 3.6 and 2.8 seconds for the 54 and 216 trial groups, but 6.9 seconds for the zero trial group. Clearly, the zero trial group was still running slowly when extinction began. Nonetheless, we must allow for some slight effect of additional rewarded trials in evaluating the remainder of the data. As may be seen, however, this effect is negligible when compared with the influence of unrewarded trials.

Perhaps the most outstanding result in Table 4.3 is the fact that each of the partially rewarded groups takes more trials, on the average, to reach the criterion of extinction than does any of the continuously rewarded groups. This is true regardless of the number of training trials given. In other words, the effect of unrewarded trials is completely different from that of rewarded trials. The impression given is of a different and unique process adding its effect to that associated with traditional reward factors.

The manner in which this different process operates can be seen a little more clearly by contrasting the various groups when the number of unrewarded trials is held constant. For the same number of unrewarded trials, variation in the per cent of reward has little or no effect on resistance to extinction. For groups having 16 non-rewards, the average trials to criterion range from 26.3 to 30.2. An analysis of variance indicates that these differences do not approach significance. Similar results are obtained for those groups that had 27 and 72 unrewarded trials. The ranges are small and the differences that exist are not significant. These results make it obvious that the usual negative correlation between percentage of reward and resistance to extinction is artifactual. It comes about because the usual procedure in such studies results in a complete confounding of the number of unrewarded trials with percentage of reward. In fact, in the present data there is a small but interesting reversal of the usual relationship. When the number of unrewarded trials is held constant, there is a tendency for those groups that received the highest percentage of reward to take slightly longer to extinguish—undoubtedly because the groups with the higher percentage receive more rewarded trials than do groups with a lower percentage. The magnitude of this effect on resistance to extinction is comparable to the differences observed among our continuously rewarded groups.

The data in Table 4.3 make it equally clear that as the number of unrewarded trials is increased, regardless of the percentage of reward involved, resistance to extinction increases markedly. Within each ratio of reward, the differences between the 16 and 72 non-reward trial groups are significant well beyond the .01 level. To judge the magnitude of this effect, one must recall that it takes continuously rewarded animals about 20 trials, on the average, to reach the criterion of extinction. With only 16 non-rewards, this increases to slightly under 30, or about half again as much. With 72 non-rewards, the average increases to approximately 50 trials, or two and one-half times that shown by continuously rewarded animals. In light of these results, one must conclude that the process by means of which partial reward increases resistance to extinction is a process that occurs on unrewarded trials. Furthermore, this effect accumulates as the number of such trials increases. For all practical purposes, in our data this effect is independent of any interaction between rewarded and unrewarded trials.

The results discussed so far have been plotted in Figure 4.1. The black circles represent 67 per cent reward, the crossed circles 50 per cent reward, and the open ones 33 per cent reward. For the 100 per cent reward groups, that is, the ones with zero unrewarded trials, the black, crossed, and open circles represent the groups having 216, 54, and 0 trials in addition to preliminary training. A glance at this figure makes it apparent that the ratio of reward during acquisition has only a negligible effect.

It is interesting, and rather surprising, that we obtain no effect whatever that might be attributed to the contrast between acquisition and extinction, the notion underlying any discrimination hypothesis that rests heavily on the familiarity the animal acquires with the relative frequencies of rewarded and unrewarded trials. From such a hypothesis, it could be argued that groups on different ratios of reward might not differ in resistance to extinction when each has received only a few unrewarded trials, since, with so few training trials, the various ratios of reward would not have been distinguished. Thus, all groups might act alike when tested on extinction. However, with large numbers of trials each group should be rather certain about the characteristics of the ratio it was on. This line of argument implies that the differences in Figure 4.1 among the various ratio of reward groups should begin to increase as the number of unrewarded trials increases. It is perfectly clear, however, that this does not occur. The magnitudes of these differences are practically indistinguishable throughout the range studied. And certainly 72 unrewarded trials (which means that even the 33 per cent reward group has been on this schedule for 108 trials) is long enough for an animal to be fairly certain about the ratios involved.

TABLE 4.4

AVERAGE RUNNING TIMES (IN SECONDS) BY RATIO
OF REWARD (EXPERIMENT 5)

|  | Reward Schedule | | |
| --- | --- | --- | --- |
|  | 33% | 50% | 67% |
| ACQUISITION |  |  |  |
| Next to last day (6 trials) | 7.18 | 3.35 | 2.66 |
| Last day (6 trials) | 5.40 | 3.05 | 2.75 |
| EXTINCTION |  |  |  |
| Trials 1–3 | 6.29 | 3.77 | 2.61 |
| Trials 4–6 | 8.11 | 6.45 | 5.38 |
| Trials 7–9 | 13.70 | 9.15 | 9.52 |
| Trials 10–12 | 18.92 | 11.23 | 13.03 |
| Trials 13–15 | 24.91 | 20.93 | 17.69 |
| Trials 16–18 | 26.09 | 22.93 | 21.46 |

It is possible, however, that we do not see the effect of ratio of reward because we are looking at the data in a rather gross manner. The effects of contrast with acquisition may show themselves only early in a series of extinction trials. To check on this, we may look at the average running times for the various groups during the initial stages of extinction.

Table 4.4 presents the data on the average running times for each percentage of reward condition. All groups having the same percentage of reward have been pooled for this purpose without regard to the number of unrewarded trials. In this way we can see the effect of percentage of reward when the average number of unrewarded trials is the same (except for the 67 per cent reward schedule where the condition of 27 unrewarded trials is missing). The first two rows of Table 4.4 are the average running times for the final two days of acquisition, each number being based on 6 trials. The last six rows are the averages for successive sets of 3 trials during the first 18 trials of extinction. The same data are presented graphically in Figure 4.2. Clearly, there is no difference in the rate of extinction during early extinction trials for the three different ratio of reward groups. The extinction curves for all three conditions tend to be parallel. Thus, even in the initial stages of extinction, the ratio of reward

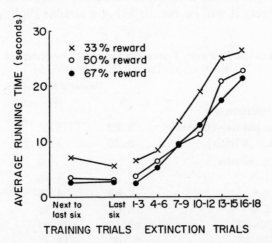

FIG. 4.2.—AVERAGE RUNNING TIME BY RATIO OF REWARD (EXPERIMENT 5)

is quite unimportant in determining the rate of extinction. These data fail to support any notion about contrast effects. Certainly, if such contrast played a role in determining this behavior, we would anticipate some difference in the rate of extinction between the 33 per cent and 67 per cent reward groups for at least the first 9 to 12 trials. During training the 67 per cent reward groups experienced only two unrewarded trials each day whereas the 33 per cent reward groups experienced four such trials a day. From any contrast hypothesis, one should anticipate that the fourth, fifth, and sixth extinction trials would have a much greater impact on the 67 per cent than on the 33 per cent animals. Similarly, the next three to six trials should augment this difference. With the restricted "random" schedules of rewards used in training these groups, these trials should clearly inform the 67 per cent animals that conditions have changed. The performance data on these trials, however, provide no evidence that such an effect occurs.

It is also interesting to note that, when the number of unrewarded trials are equated as in these data, there is a direct relationship between the running speeds during acquisition and extinction. The animals trained with 33 per cent reward are definitely slower at the end of training than are the other animals. This difference is maintained throughout the first 18 trials of extinction. It will be recalled that a similar slight difference

TABLE 4.5

AVERAGE RUNNING TIMES (IN SECONDS) BY NUMBER OF
UNREWARDED TRIALS (EXPERIMENT 5)

|  | Number of Non-Rewards | | |
|---|---|---|---|
|  | 16 | 27 | 72 |
| ACQUISITION |  |  |  |
| Next to last day (6 trials) | 3.29 | 5.35 | 5.74 |
| Last day (6 trials) | 3.26 | 3.99 | 4.54 |
| EXTINCTION |  |  |  |
| Trials 1–3 | 3.94 | 4.75 | 4.97 |
| Trials 4–6 | 7.82 | 4.26 | 7.61 |
| Trials 7–9 | 16.04 | 9.71 | 7.31 |
| Trials 10–12 | 22.48 | 13.60 | 8.27 |
| Trials 13–15 | 34.07 | 16.41 | 13.79 |
| Trials 16–18 | 43.25 | 18.61 | 9.16 |

was found in the number of trials required to reach the criterion of extinction.

Finally, we need to look briefly at the data on running times during the initial trials of extinction when the groups are combined according to the number of unrewarded trials. These data are presented in Table 4.5 and Figure 4.3. It is apparent that the number of unrewarded trials makes an all-important difference in the rate of extinction. The groups with the fewest unrewarded trials extinguish the most rapidly, and those with the most unrewarded trials extinguish the least rapidly. This differentiation begins on the first days of extinction and is very marked by the ninth trial. Thus, the differences we noted in terms of average trials to a criterion of extinction are characteristic, and not something that only show up late in the extinction process.

In summary, the results of this study lend support to two implications from dissonance theory. They support the idea, first, that the processes producing increased resistance to extinction after partial reward occur primarily on the unrewarded trial itself and, second, that these dissonance reduction effects

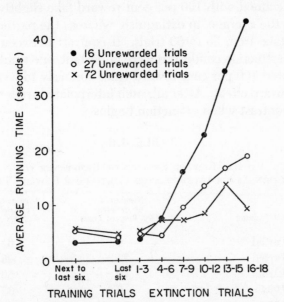

FIG. 4.3.—AVERAGE RUNNING TIME BY NUMBER OF UNREWARDED TRIALS (EXPERIMENT 5)

are cumulative. In addition, this study makes untenable a variety of other explanations of the partial reward effect. Any explanation that relies, in whole or in part, on the contrast between acquisition and extinction trials is no longer tenable.

Our confidence in dismissing such explanations is increased because of an additional study reported by Theios (1961). He tested the effects on resistance to extinction of interpolating a series of 100 per cent rewarded trials between the partial reward training and the extinction test. Specifically, Theios tested the resistance to extinction of three identically trained partial reward groups. One group was extinguished immediately after partial reward training; another had 25 additional trials with 100 per cent reward before extinction; and a third had 70 such 100 per cent rewarded trials between partial reward training and extinction. In addition, two control groups which received only 100 per cent reward were run.

Table 4.6 presents the results of this experiment. It is clear that the interpolation of continuously rewarded trials between partial reward training and extinction has little or no effect. Animals trained with 100 per cent reward take slightly over 30 trials, on the average, to extinguish, whereas the partial reward animals take from 50 to 66 trials. If contrast between acquisition and extinction conditions were important, one would expect interpolated 100 per cent reward trials seriously to weaken the partial reward effect. After all, such interpolated trials make for a sharp contrast when extinction begins.

TABLE 4.6

PARTIAL REWARD EFFECTS ON RESISTANCE TO
EXTINCTION AFTER INTERPOLATED CONTINUOUS REWARD TRIALS[*]

| Original Training | Number of Interpolated 100% Reward Trials | Average Number of Trials to Extinction |
|---|---|---|
| Partial | 0 | 61 |
| Partial | 25 | 66 |
| Partial | 70 | 50 |
| 100% | 0 | 33 |
| 100% | 70 | 31 |

[*] From Theios (1961).

## The Relation of Dissonance to Non-Reward

Theoretically, not all instances of absence of reward should produce dissonance. Our formulation implies that if an animal performs an act, even though it is very effortful, and finds an adequate reward, little or no dissonance is introduced. On the other hand, if the animal performs the act and does not find a reward, dissonance is aroused and dissonance reduction occurs. The crux of this formulation is this: the experiencing of non-reward per se is not sufficient to arouse dissonance. It is only when an animal performs an act in the expectation of being rewarded that not obtaining the reward generates any dissonance. To add weight to our theoretical interpretation it would be useful to show that experience with non-reward, if such experience fails to produce dissonance, does not increase resistance to extinction.

To demonstrate this, we need a situation in which an animal experiences occasional non-rewards in a goal box, the non-rewards coming only on occasions when it has not performed any definite act oriented toward getting food and thus does not expect food. Under these circumstances, no dissonance should be aroused since the absence of food is not dissonant with the animal's behavior. Consequently, no extra attractions should develop. In an attempt to show this, we designed and ran the following study.

## Experiment 6.—Placing vs. Partial Reward Effects

The apparatus for this experiment was an 8-foot-long enclosed runway leading to a black goal box. A delivery tube was centered above the food dish so that, on rewarded trials, a pellet of wet mash could be dropped after the animal had entered the goal box. Three hurdles, each 3 inches high, were spaced evenly throughout the alley.

Three groups of rats, approximately ninety days old at the beginning of the experiment, were trained on this apparatus. There were 12 animals in each group, half males and half females. A 100 per cent reward group was rewarded on each trial; a 50 per cent reward group was rewarded on half the trials and retained in the goal box for 20 seconds without food on the other half. The third group, a placed group, was trained in an unusual fashion. These animals ran the alley and found food on half their trials just as did the 50 per cent reward group. On the other half of the trials, however, these animals did not run the alley. Instead they were placed directly in the goal box, immediately in front of the entrance door, and then retained there for 20 seconds without food. Thus, their experiences in the goal box were directly comparable to those of the partially rewarded animals. However, whenever these animals ran the alley this act of running was rewarded. They were unlike the partially rewarded animals in that, for the placed group, non-reward was not dissonance producing because very quickly these animals learned not to expect food when placed in the goal box.

All animals were tamed and placed on a 22-hour deprivation schedule. They were given 4 preliminary trials of eating in the goal box, followed by 6 rewarded trials during which the hurdles were gradually increased to their full height. Thereafter, all animals were given 6 trials a day, spaced at least 15 minutes apart, for a total of 72 training trials. For the 50 per cent reward animals, 3 of these trials each day were unrewarded, occurring in an unpredictable order. These same 3 trials were unrewarded for the placed group.

This training was followed by 48 extinction trials for all animals, again at the rate of 6 a day, with at least 15 minutes between trials. Running times from the opening of the start box door until entrance into the goal box were taken on each trial both during training and extinction. If an animal had not entered the goal box within 90 seconds, it was removed from the apparatus. During the course of the experiment one animal in the placed group died, leaving only 11. By the end of training all three groups were running about equally fast. On unrewarded trials, the placed group showed evidence that it did not look for food.

Table 4.7 presents the data for the three groups on the average number of trials required to reach a criterion of extinction of two 60-second trials, not necessarily consecutive. This arbitrary criterion was chosen since all animals did reach it within

TABLE 4.7

THE EFFECTS OF PLACING VS. PARTIAL REWARD
ON RESISTANCE TO EXTINCTION (EXPERIMENT 6)

| Training Condition | Number of Trials to Extinction |
|---|---|
| 50% Reward (N = 12) | 27.8 |
| Placed (N = 11) | 18.2 |
| 100% Reward (N = 12) | 20.9 |

the 48 extinction trials. It may be seen in the table that the usual effect of partial reward is obtained. The 50 per cent reward group requires 27.8 trials whereas the 100 per cent reward group requires only 20.9 trials to extinguish. This difference is significant at the .05 level. Looking at the data for the placed group, we find that the mere experience of being in the food compartment without food does not increase resistance to extinction. The placed group extinguishes in 18.2 trials, in contrast to the 27.8 trials of the 50 per cent group, again a difference significant at the .05 level. Thus, there is no evidence that extra attractions for a situation develop merely because nonreward experiences are associated with it. Resistance to extinction is increased only if non-reward signifies that the performance of a given action is not justified, that is, if dissonance is introduced.

We willingly grant that the results of this study can be interpreted in a number of different ways. The important question, however, is whether the mere experience of non-reward in the goal box is sufficient to build up resistance to extinction, or whether this experience has to disconfirm an expectancy. The results tend to confirm the assumption we are making that dissonance and dissonance reduction do not occur in the former case.

*Summary*

The evidence in this chapter supports three basic assumptions underlying our dissonance explanation of partial reward effects on resistance to extinction. (1) we have shown that the crucial factor is the unrewarded trial. The percentage of reward is of little or no consequence. (2) We have shown that the effect of these non-rewards is cumulative. When groups are equated on number of unrewarded trials, regardless of percentage of reward, they show comparable magnitudes of resistance to extinction. (3) We have demonstrated that it is not the experience of non-reward per se that is crucial. Rather, it is only when this experience is related to the expectation of reward that it has any influence on resistance to extinction. This implies that dissonance and dissonance reduction occur only when the animal has taken an action and then finds that this action is not justified by its consequences.

What has been shown for partial reward procedures should also apply to delay of reward and effort expenditure. In these instances the delay, or the effort expended, introduces dissonance rather than expecting and not obtaining reward. Resistance to extinction should be an increasing function of the number of such dissonance-producing trials. At present there are no data in the literature strictly relevant to this issue, although some inferences can be made in the case of delay of reward from the study done by Wike and McNamara (1957). They gave all of their groups an equal number of training trials, but they varied the percentage of trials on which the reward was delayed. Resistance to extinction increased directly as the percentage of these delay trials increased. In their study, of course, the number of delay trials and the percentage of delay were directly correlated. Thus, while they interpret the results as though the percentage were the crucial variable, it is more probable in terms of what we have shown in this chapter that the number of such delay experiences is the primary variable.

# 5

# The Effects of a
# Zero Reward Schedule

In the previous chapter, the outstanding conclusion was that partial reward effects depend primarily on the absolute number rather than the percentage of unrewarded trials. There is, unfortunately, one ambiguity in the interpretation of these findings: all of the experimental tests have involved situations in which the animal has experienced both reward and non-reward in exactly the same place. Consequently, it is possible to frame any number of explanations that hinge on this fact. For instance, Amsel's frustration hypothesis (1958) assumes that the rewarded trials are necessary to enable the animal to establish an anticipatory goal response. On unrewarded trials, the conjunction of these anticipatory goal responses and the absence of reward result in the arousal of frustration. Thus, a specific kind of interaction between rewarded and unrewarded trials is central in this hypothesis.

From our point of view, dissonance will be aroused, and dissonance reduction will take place, as long as the animal can be induced to continue performing a motivated act even though a reward is never obtained. Theoretically, extra attractions would develop even if an animal were trained on a zero reward schedule, that is, one on which it repeatedly performs an act but is never rewarded for it. If such a performance could be shown, it would be very strong evidence for the dissonance explanation and at the same time would rule out alternative interpretations such as the one suggested by Amsel. Obviously, we cannot train an animal to perform an act consistently if there are no incentives at all. We can, however, approximate this situation, as we shall see later, by inducing an animal to go consistently to a place that is never *directly* associated with reward. We shall refer to such an approximation as a "zero reward" situation.

Any experiment that would permit us to say, unequivocally, that a zero reward schedule had resulted in extra attractions must face, and solve, certain problems. Let us assume that we have trained an animal to perform an act repeatedly and that this act has never been directly rewarded. As a consequence, dissonance has been introduced in each trial, and the resulting dissonance reduction has led to the discovery of extra attractions in the situation. The initial problem is how we demonstrate that these extra attractions are present, that is, against what base line do we compare the performance of this animal? Ideally, we should like a control animal for whom both the activity and the situation are familiar but neutral in attractiveness. Unfamiliarity might well result in emotional factors that would inhibit the animal's performance. Clearly, however, this combination of neutral attractiveness with familiarity can never be produced with any assurance. If experience with the activity and situation is given in conjunction with reward, there is every reason to expect that some attractiveness, as the result of secondary reward, will develop. If this experience is given in the absence of reward, but under conditions that preclude the operation of dissonance reduction, there is every reason to expect that some negative incentive value will result. Thus, a base line of neutral attractiveness is probably unattainable.

The inevitable conclusion is that we must contrast our zero reward animal with one that has experienced a 100 per cent reward schedule. This ensures equal familiarity for both animals but limits us to contrasting two forms of attractiveness, that based on dissonance reduction versus that based on secondary reward. Granted this necessity, it is clear that only one type of empirical outcome has an unambiguous interpretation from the point of view of dissonance theory. If the zero reward animal persists longer during extinction than the 100 per cent reward animal, some attractiveness obviously has developed as a result of dissonance reduction.

Another condition must also be fulfilled before the results of a zero reward schedule are interpretable from the point of view of dissonance reduction. First of all, as we have emphasized previously, the training situation must be so arranged that the animal does not change its behavior. Any indication that the animal is refusing to run counterindicates the building up of extra attractions. Thus, something must be provided in the experimental situation which will guarantee that the animal continues to run.

The main type of evidence available on this question of zero reward effects is illustrated by a recent study by Marx (1960). He ran a single group of animals on a runway. Three different end boxes were used, each on a third of the trials, but only one of these ever contained food. The animals were thus trained on a 33 per cent reward schedule, the reward being associated with only one end box. Of the various subgroups on which he conducted extinction tests, two are of particular interest to us. One of these groups had the formerly rewarded end box present during extinction while the other had one of the unrewarded ones. The former group required 45.7 trials to reach a criterion of extinction whereas the latter required 50.7 trials. Although this difference does not reach statistical significance, it does indicate that non-reward produced effects as strong as those attributable to secondary reward. It must be admitted, however, that the results are ambiguous for our purposes, for the training situation permitted the animal to anticipate which end box was present on any trial. In fact, the training data indicate that the animals were able to establish a discrimination between the rewarded and unrewarded trials. Such discrimination—that is, not expecting reward on unrewarded trials—would retard the development of any extra attractions.

This development of discrimination was partially controlled in a study done by Bitterman, Feddersen, and Tyler (1953). Their apparatus consisted of a runway ending in a gap that the animal had to jump before it could enter the goal box. At the entrance to the goal box there was a cardboard door which prevented the animal from seeing the interior of the box while jumping. All animals in the study were given 10 massed training trials a day for 10 days. Half of these trials were rewarded and half were not rewarded. The interior of the goal box was one color (e.g., black) on rewarded trials and a different color (e.g., white) on unrewarded trials. Thus, the first color should have acquired secondary reward value because it was always associated with primary reward; the second color, of course, should not have acquired secondary reward value. But, if dissonance reduction occurred, this second color should have become an incentive in its own right because the animal consistently expended considerable effort to go there without any reward to justify this behavior. The reason the animal continued in this nonsensical behavior is obvious: at the time it jumped the gap it was unaware, because of the cardboard door, that the unrewarded box was present. But, having performed the act and then not having been rewarded for it, it should have experienced dissonance.

At the completion of training the animals were divided into two groups for extinction. The control group ran to the goal box associated with reward whereas the experimental group ran to the one associated with non-reward. Extinction was significantly slower for the experimental group running to the unrewarded box than for the control group running to the rewarded one. Elam, Tyler, and Bitterman (1954) confirmed these results in a second study using spaced trials during both training and extinction. Thus, on the basis of these studies there is evidence that attractions do develop in the goal box during a zero reward schedule.

The results of these studies by Bitterman and his colleagues seemed to offer such dramatic support for dissonance theory that it appeared worth while to confirm and extend them. As a first step, we replicated the second of the above studies, using more widely spaced trials, a slightly shorter runway, and a larger number of training trials. Ten animals were run in each extinction condition. Our results showed that both groups took equally long to extinguish. There was no indication of a significant difference between them. We repeated our study with 20 more rats and again got the same outcome. Thus, our own results are more in line with those reported by Marx (1960). Although our studies indicated that zero reward produces effects on extinction that are as strong as those ascribable to secondary reward, we were unable to reproduce the dramatic difference reported by Bitterman and his coworkers. We have no clear explanation of this difference in outcome.

This failure to replicate a difference favoring the zero reward group is bothersome. Clearly, it would be valuable to construct an experimental situation in which the Bitterman result could be produced with greater stability. In an attempt to do so we decided to compare two independent groups both voluntarily going to a given place. One of these groups would always be rewarded, while the other would never be rewarded. There is, of course, an obvious technical problem that must be solved in order to do such an experiment: How can one design a procedure that will induce an animal to continue engaging in an action for which it has never been rewarded and for which it never is rewarded? One could, of course, force the animal by physically pushing it or by compelling it to engage in the activity in order to avoid some noxious stimulation. But neither of these procedures satisfies our requirements. In the former case the animal is not voluntarily engaging in the activity, and, in the latter case, escaping the noxious stimulation is every bit as good as being rewarded. The technical problem does not, in this form, really seem capable of solution. To require an animal to perform an act for no reason whatsoever is, perhaps, impossible in principle.

In order to design an experiment to meet the requirements we have stated it is obviously necessary to make some compromises. The compromise we decided on, which would allow us to solve the technical problems and still obtain data that were meaningful with respect to the question of zero reward, was to use a variation of a delay of reward experiment. Animals could be run under conditions of delay—that is, on every trial they would be delayed for a period of time in a mid-box before being allowed to continue to an end box where food would be obtained. One could then test, during "extinction," their willingness to continue running just to the mid-box, a place where they had been delayed en route to food and never rewarded.

From the existing literature, of course, we already know that such delay will increase resistance to extinction when extinction trials are run from the start box to the end box. Such data, although they support the dissonance formulation, are not conclusive for the question of zero reward. According to our formulation, the dissonance produced by the delay experience is reduced in at least two ways—in conjunction with the situation in which the delay occurs, and in connection with things experienced immediately after the delay. Thus, the end box has acquired some extra attraction even though delay has occurred prior to it and resistance to extinction is increased. Such results, however, are not completely decisive for our present purposes because, after all, the animal is demonstrating increased willingness to go to a place where it has been *rewarded* (the end box), and this might be the result of some interaction between the dissonance-producing experience of delay and the reward it obtains. If, however, one could demonstrate the same increased resistance to extinction when it is running only to a mid-box, that is, to a place never associated with reward, this would tend to eliminate this ambiguity and to focus attention on the experience of non-reward itself.

*Experiment 7.—The Effect of a Zero Reward Schedule*

The specific design of the experiment we conducted was as follows. The apparatus consisted of an L-shaped runway. The first stem, painted gray, was 4 feet 10 inches long, the first 10 inches being the start box. Spaced evenly throughout the runway were four 3-inch-high hurdles. This runway opened into an unpainted mid-box, at the right rear corner of which was an exit passage at right angles to the first runway. The second runway, painted black, extended for 3 feet beyond the exit passage. No hurdles were present. It opened into a black end box, 8 inches wide, 12 inches long, and 5 inches deep—dimensions very different from those of the mid-box.

Fifty-four albino rats, half males and half females, were tamed and then placed on a 22-hour food-deprivation schedule which was maintained throughout the experiment. After becoming adapted to eating pellets of wet mash in the end box, all animals were given 20 runs, spaced over six days, from the start box to the end box. During this period the hurdles were introduced and gradually raised to full height. On these runs 36 of the animals found a pellet of food in both the mid-box and the end box. The other 18 animals were never rewarded in the mid-box. Instead, they were delayed there for an interval which was gradually increased until, on the last two trials, the delay was 20 seconds. These animals were rewarded, however, on reaching the end box.

At this stage the 36 animals that had been fed in the mid-box were further divided into two groups of 18 each. For the remainder of their training, one of these groups, the 100 per cent group, continued to find food in the mid-box on every trial. As soon as they turned away from the food dish, the exit door was opened. The other group, a 50 per cent group, found food in the mid-box on only half the trials. On the other half, these animals were delayed there without food for 20 seconds before the exit door was opened. The third group, a zero per cent group, continued to be delayed in the mid-box for 20 seconds without food on every trial. The 100 per cent and 50 per cent groups required about 20 seconds to eat the food in the mid-box. On these rewarded trials, the exit door was opened as soon as they turned away from the food dish. All animals, of course, found food in the end box on every trial. Thus, the three groups differed only in the percentage of times each found food in the mid-box.

These training trials were given at the rate of 5 a day for 16 days. There were at least 30 minutes between each trial. Running times were taken from the opening of the start box door until the animal entered the mid-box. At the end of training, all groups were given extinction trials. These trials were run from the start box to the mid-box only. In the latter, the animal was retained for 20 seconds without food and then returned to its home cage. If an animal failed to enter the mid-box within 120 seconds, it was taken out of the apparatus. The criterion of extinction was 5 such trials, not necessarily consecutive. A maximum of 90 extinction trials were run at the rate of 5 a day, with at least 30 minutes between trials. One animal in the 50 per cent group died during training.

From our theoretical point of view, we can summarize the procedure as follows: The second runway, and the end box in which all animals were rewarded every trial, can be regarded as having nothing to do with the experiment except for providing the conditions under which all animals would continue to perform the activity during training. In other words, reward in the end box was the thing that "tricked" the zero per cent group into continuing to respond. The experiment proper is concerned only with the first part of the apparatus, namely, start box, runway, and mid-box. Confining our attention to this part of the apparatus, our experimental procedures have produced three groups—a 100 per cent reward group, a 50 per cent reward group, and a zero per cent reward group.

Let us look at the results. If our theory is correct, the zero per cent group, having had the largest number of unrewarded experiences, should be the slowest to extinguish. The comparison between the 100 per cent and 50 per cent groups should, of course, show the usual effect of partial reward.

The first data that we shall examine are the average number of trials to a criterion of extinction. It will be recalled that the animals were removed from the apparatus if they failed to enter the mid-box in 120 seconds. After 5 such trials, we stopped running the animal. Unfortunately, this proved to be much too strict a criterion of extinction. After 90 extinction trials, at which point we discontinued the experiment, there were still several animals running. Therefore, we arbitrarily chose some reasonable value with respect to which all animals had "extinguished" within the 90 trials that we ran. To be sure that the choice of criterion did not make any essential difference, we analyzed the data with respect to a number of them and found the results to be always approximately the same. The data shown in Table 5.1 are based on a criterion of 5 trials in which the animal did not enter the mid-box within 30 seconds.

A glance at the table shows that, as expected, the zero per cent reward condition had the greatest resistance to extinction. It takes this group an average of 43.6 trials to reach the criterion of extinction as compared with 37.1 trials for the 50 per cent reward group and only 28.4 trials for the 100 per cent reward

TABLE 5.1

RESISTANCE TO EXTINCTION FOR DIFFERENT
PERCENTAGE OF REWARD GROUPS (EXPERIMENT 7)

| Experimental Group | N | Average Number of Trials to Extinction |
|---|---|---|
| 100% Reward | 18 | 28.4 |
| 50% Reward | 17 | 37.1 |
| 0% Reward | 18 | 43.6 |

group. The averages of the 100 per cent reward group and the 50 per cent reward group are significantly different at the .02 level of significance. In other words, we do get the usual partial reward effect on resistance to extinction. The difference between the 50 per cent reward and zero per cent reward groups is significant at the .05 level. This seems to be sufficient demonstration that additional unrewarded experiences in a place increase the magnitude of extra attractions, and hence resistance to extinction, even if the place is one where the animal has never experienced any extrinsic reward.

The data on running time during extinction show the same effects. Figure 5.1 presents the average running times on the last day of acquisition and the first ten days of extinction. It will be noticed that the 100 per cent reward group extinguishes most quickly and the zero per cent reward group is most resistant to extinction.

There is, however, some point in examining these data on running times during extinction somewhat more closely. First of all, it is clear that the three groups of animals are not running equally fast at the end of the acquisition period. The 100 per cent reward animals have an average running time of 1.9 seconds, the 50 per cent reward animals have a time of 2.3 seconds, and the zero per cent reward animals have a rather long running time—an average of 4.2 seconds. These times are, of course, quite reasonable and consistent with the previous data we have presented for partial reward situations.

For the first two days of extinction there is not very much difference among our three experimental conditions, but after the second day the differences become very clear. The 100 per

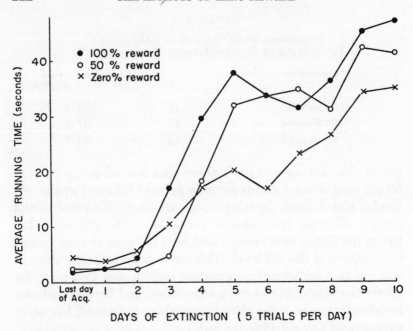

FIG. 5.1.—RATE OF EXTINCTION FOR 100 PER CENT, 50 PER CENT, AND ZERO PER CENT REWARD GROUPS (EXPERIMENT 7)

cent reward group slows considerably in a rather short period of time. By the fifth day this group has reached, and thereafter maintains, a relatively slow running speed. The 50 per cent reward group does not slow down so quickly; particularly on the third and fourth day of extinction it runs very much faster than the 100 per cent reward group. By the sixth day of extinction, however, the difference between these two groups has vanished. The zero per cent reward group, on the other hand, shows a more lasting effect. Consistent with its performance at the end of acquisition, this group starts off running more slowly than the others. By the third extinction day, however, its curve has crossed that for the 100 per cent reward animals, and by the fifth day has crossed that for the 50 per cent reward animals. These zero per cent reward animals show a very slow increase in running time. Certainly, there is no question about the greater resistance to extinction of those animals that are running to a place where they have never been rewarded.

These results, comparing a zero reward schedule with other reward schedules and using independent groups, are clear and unambiguous. They fit well with our contention that the crucial variable in prolonging extinction after partial reward is the number of unrewarded trials. The effect does not seem to be dependent upon any interaction between reward and non-reward experiences in the same place. At the same time, these results indicate that the same explanation we have used for partial effects also accounts for delay of reward effects. The design we used in this experiment is a natural extension of a delay of reward experiment. We have merely separated the place associated with delay from the place associated with reward, and then shown that the former has acquired a positive incentive value. All of this fits in neatly with a dissonance interpretation.

It may have occurred to the reader that the results of this zero reward experiment, considered in isolation, can be interpreted in terms of similarity between acquisition and extinction conditions. After all, this similarity is greatest for the zero per cent reward group and least for the 100 per cent reward group. However, these results must not be considered alone and apart from other findings. It must be remembered that the results of Experiment 5, on the cumulative aspects of dissonance reduction, demonstrated unequivocally that similarity between acquisition and extinction conditions is not an important variable in increasing resistance to extinction. Once having disposed of this variable, we certainly do not want to revive it. We should, of course, like to have a unitary explanation for all the relevant data.

There is, however, a possible alternative explanation that we should consider seriously at this point. This comes from the theory proposed by Amsel (1958), who hypothesizes that frustration results in increased drive. He, and others, have presented data demonstrating that after the frustration of not having been fed when expecting food, the organism reacts with intensified vigor. The usual type of situation in which this finding has been reported closely resembles the experiment we have described in this chapter. There are usually a start box, alley, mid-box, second alley, and end box. The animals are trained to run to the mid-box, eat, then run to the end box and eat again. There are usually two groups, which are treated differently. One group continues to find food in both boxes whereas the other finds food in the mid-box only on some of the trials. The finding is that, after an unrewarded mid-box experience, the animal runs faster in the second alley.

If one accepts this finding, which has been reported sufficiently often so that it is undoubtedly correct, and if one accepts frustration as the explanation, the question arises of whether the phenomenon of increased resistance to extinction could be the result of the same increased vigor following frustration. Fortunately, the theory of frustration drive as stated by Amsel is specific enough to allow us to answer this question. According to his formulation, frustration is aroused if the animal expects food and does not obtain it. Thus, according to his theory, an animal that is partially rewarded in the mid-box experiences frustration, but an animal that is never rewarded in the mid-box, and consequently has never learned to expect food there, does not experience frustration and should show no increased vigor.

There is a very nice experiment by Wagner (1959) which tests this implication of the Amsel formulation of frustration drive. In this experiment Wagner used the usual type of apparatus described above. He ran three groups of animals, a group that was always rewarded in the mid-box, a group that was partially rewarded in the mid-box, and a group that was never rewarded in the mid-box. In other words, the three groups that he ran exactly parallel our three groups in the experiment we described in this chapter.

The most important measure that Wagner obtained in his experiment was the one customarily used in relation to Amsel's theory, namely, speed of running the second alley. His findings, comparing the 100 per cent mid-box reward group and the partial mid-box reward group, wholly confirm earlier work on this effect. On rewarded mid-box trials the partial reward group ran the second alley at about the same speed as the 100 per cent reward animals, but on unrewarded mid-box trials it ran faster in the second alley. The results that Wagner obtained for his zero reward group are also consistent in every way with Amsel's theory: the zero reward group, never having experienced the frustration of expecting food and not obtaining it in the mid-box, does *not* run faster in the second alley.

At the same time that this study confirms the theory of Amsel in relation to what does and does not arouse frustration, it also makes it impossible to use that same theory to explain the increased resistance to extinction in the experiment we reported in this chapter. It will be recalled that in our experiment the zero per cent reward group showed the greatest resistance to extinction, and the 50 per cent reward group showed results midway between the zero and 100 per cent reward groups. In other words, if frustration and frustration drive were causing the increased resistance to extinction, one would have to maintain that the zero per cent reward group experienced the greatest amount of frustration and had the strongest frustration drive. The Wagner experiment shows clearly, however, that a zero per cent reward group experiences no frustration and shows no frustration drive in the Amsel sense. Thus it is clear that these two phenomena, namely, greater speed of running in the second alley after non-reward and greater resistance to extinction after unrewarded experiences, cannot possibly be explained by the same theory.

In summary, we have shown that a mixture of rewards and non-rewards is not necessary for the partial reward effect on resistance to extinction. The number of unrewarded experiences is crucial, and a zero per cent reward schedule is, of course, maximally effective in prolonging extinction.

In designing our zero reward experiment, in order to motivate the animals to run, a delay of reward situation was employed. It is clear that delay of reward has the same cumulative effects as partial reward, which dissonance theory would imply.

Our experimental findings, in conjunction with those reported by Wagner (1959), have enabled us to rule out Amsel's frustration theory as a possible explanation for increased resistance to extinction. Of course, we have not ruled out all possible theoretical formulations using the concept "frustration." The only thing one can do is to examine any specific formulation of "frustration" as it is offered.

# 6

# The Effect of Weak Drive States

The present dissonance reduction explanation of prolonged extinction effects implies certain suggestions about the role of motivation. Let us review, briefly, what was said about motivation in Chapter 2. The dominant drive of the animal during acquisition was said to determine, in part, the amount of dissonance experienced and also, in part, the extent to which this dissonance can be reduced by finding extra attractions in the situation.

The strength of motivation during acquisition determines the importance to the animal of the consequences of its action. We have said that if a hungry animal performs an act and is rewarded with food, the action and its consequence are consonant with each other. The weight, or importance, this consonant relationship has in determining the animal's behavior depends, however, upon the strength of its motivation: if the animal is very hungry, this consonant relationship has considerable weight, but if the animal is less motivated, it has correspondingly less weight. This assumption is, of course, much the same as that underlying most theories of learning. It implies that the animal is more willing to run when highly motivated. In the present context, however, motivation also has an effect in determining the amount of dissonance that is aroused when the consequences of an action fail to justify it. For instance, if an animal performs an act in order to obtain food and fails to find food, it will have experienced more dissonance if it is highly motivated than if it is only slightly so. Thus, in a partial reward situation, for example, the amount of dissonance aroused on an unrewarded trial is a direct function of the degree of hunger motivation. This in turn determines the pressure on the animal to reduce the dissonance through the discovery of extra attractions in the situation. Consequently, the stronger the dominant motivation the greater is the pressure to discover extra attractions in the situation whenever dissonance is aroused by absence or delay of reward.

We also attributed a second function to the dominant motivation. Largely on intuitive grounds, we assumed that the stronger the dominant motivation, the harder it would be for the animal actually to discover extra attractions in the situation that would justify its behavior. It will be remembered that these extra attractions satisfy subordinate motivations the animal may have at the time dissonance is aroused. The ease with which the animal can discover such attractions will therefore depend, in part, on the number and strength of these subordinate motivations. In light of what is known about drive interactions, it seems reasonable to assume that subordinate motivations would be weaker and less salient if the dominant motivation were very strong than if it were weak. We thus come to the conclusion that whereas the pressure to find extra attractions increases with increasing motivation, the possibility of finding them decreases. In the remainder of this chapter we shall present experimental evidence relevant to the effect of different levels of motivation.

## The Effect of Weak Motivation During Acquisition

It is clear from the above review of how motivations interact with dissonance and dissonance reduction that two opposing processes occur during acquisition for partially rewarded animals. If the dominant motivation is strong, there is considerable dissonance but poor dissonance reduction; if the dominant motivation is weak, there is less dissonance but good dissonance reduction.

Despite this ambiguity resulting from the presence of two counteracting processes, we can state one clear implication from dissonance theory: raising or lowering the level of motivation during acquisition should have no appreciable effect on the difference in resistance to extinction between a 100 per cent reward group and a partial reward group. In other words, we are inclined to expect that partial reward should lead to increased resistance to extinction even under conditions of minimal motivation. Because there were no data available on this point, we carried out a small experiment to test whether or not the partial reward effect would be obtained when animals were weakly motivated during acquisition.

## Experiment 8.—Partial Reward Effects Under Weak Motivation

Twenty-four rats, half of them males and half females, were used in this study. After being tamed, they were placed on a 22-hour food-deprivation schedule. During the next 5 days they were given preliminary training in an apparatus consisting of a 4-foot alley containing three hurdles, each 3 inches high, spaced at equal distances in the alley. In preliminary training they were accustomed to running the alley and finding, in the goal box, a sugar-coated pellet of breakfast food. During these trials the hurdles in the alley were gradually raised to their full height.

After preliminary training, all animals were taken off their deprivation schedule and given continuous access to regular laboratory food pellets in their home cages. This continued throughout the rest of the experiment. Thus, the only motivation the animals had during training and extinction was based on their liking for the sugar-coated pellet over and above any need for food. This was considered to be a minimal level of motivation, for the animals were certainly never hungry.

After an intervening 2-day period, the animals were divided into two groups, equated on the basis of their preliminary running times. All animals were then given 6 trials a day, spaced at least 15 minutes apart, for the next 20 days. One group was run on a 100 per cent reward schedule and the other on a 50 per cent reward schedule. On unrewarded trials, the 50 per cent reward animals were left in the goal box for 20 seconds. Two animals in each group were eliminated during training because of continued refusals to run or to eat, leaving only 10 animals in each group. All animals were then given extinction trials spaced at least 15 minutes apart. The criterion of extinction employed was three trials, not necessarily consecutive, on which the animal failed to enter the goal box within 180 seconds. On all other trials they were left in the goal box for 20 seconds.

On the last day of training, the 100 per cent reward group averaged 4.7 seconds per trial and the 50 per cent reward group, 8.1 seconds. These are relatively slow times for this apparatus and were to be expected under such low motivation conditions. Nonetheless, each of these animals ate the pellet each time it was available during acquisition. It should also be noted that the difference in times is in the same direction and of the same relative magnitude as that usually found in contrasts between continuously and partially rewarded animals.

The partially rewarded group proved more resistant to extinction. The number of trials to the criterion of extinction was 24.9 trials for the 100 per cent reward group and 32.5 for the 50 per cent reward group, a difference that is significant between the .05 and .10 levels. It is clear that the partial reward effect is found even though a minimal level of motivation is present during acquisition and extinction. Thus, we have some evidence for the notion that, even though very little dissonance was experienced on unrewarded trials, it was relatively easy for the animal to reduce it under conditions of low motivation.

It is convenient, at this point, to examine the implications of these data for theories which depend heavily on the unpleasant or frustrating aspects of unrewarded trials, to which, during the course of acquisition, the animal "adapts" in one way or another. Such theories should anticipate that, under very weak motivation, the partial reward effect would disappear or, at least, be greatly reduced, since an unrewarded trial cannot be very unpleasant when the animal is not hungry. If there is little unpleasantness, it is difficult to see how "adaptation" to such unpleasantness can help increase resistance to extinction.

The experiments to be reported next, using strong motivation during acquisition and weak motivation during extinction, also pose problems for these other theories. If the "adaptation" to frustration during acquisition is a major process, then it is not immediately clear why it should affect extinction behavior when the animal is not hungry and, hence, is no longer suffering the same frustrations. Thus, although our data seem to fit in well with the theory concerning the development of extra attractions, they seem to provide difficulty for some alternative interpretations.

## The Effect of Weak Motivation During Extinction

Although, as we have seen, there is ambiguity concerning the effects of motivation variation during acquisition, there are clear implications concerning the effects of differences in motivation during extinction. We can expect that the influence of extra attractions will tend to be more pronounced when extinction is run under conditions of low motivation than when it is run under conditions of high motivation. The basis for this expectation can be described briefly.

Suppose two groups of animals are trained under high motivation, one with a 100 per cent reward schedule and the other with a partial reward schedule. Suppose, further, that the motivational level is reduced to a minimum in both groups before extinction is run. The 100 per cent reward group should still extinguish fairly rapidly. The reduction in motivation should decrease its willingness to run in search of a food reward, and the absence of any extra attractions for this group means that it has little other incentive for running.

According to our formulation, however, the picture for partially rewarded animals should be considerably different. The reduction in motivation should, of course, decrease their initial willingness to run, just as for 100 per cent reward animals, but it must be remembered that part of the incentive for these animals is the extra attractions they discovered during acquisition— satisfiers, as it were, for subordinate motivations. Consequently, as long as the situation is not changed and as long as these subordinate motivations continue to operate during the extinction trials, these animals have some justification for running. In other words, the extra attractions which have been built up through dissonance reduction tend to form an intrinsic and stable group of incentives for the animal.

Remembering that (1) because of low motivation, the partially rewarded animals would experience minimal dissonance during the extinction trials, and remembering also that (2) they have some justification for running because of the extra attractions they have developed in the situation, one is led to an interesting implication. It is conceivable that these animals would show little if any evidence of extinction except for the initial decrease in willingness to run. This possibility was so intriguing that it was well worth checking.

*Experiment 9.—Comparison of Zero and Continuous Reward Groups Extinguished Under Low Motivation*

We designed an experiment to see (1) whether a partially rewarded group persists longer than one that has been continuously rewarded, both trained when hungry but extinguished under minimal motivation, and (2) whether, under these conditions, a partially rewarded group shows any evidence of an extinction process. Two groups of animals were trained under the usual motivational conditions, one with continuous reward and the other with zero reward—the latter, of course, represents the extreme of a partial reward schedule. We then tested both of them on extinction trials while they were not hungry.

The procedure that we employed was an exact repetition, using the same apparatus, of the acquisition conditions of Experiment 7, described in Chapter 5, for two of the three groups of that study, namely, the 100 per cent and the zero per cent reward groups; the 50 per cent reward group of the previous experiment was not duplicated in the present one since it was felt to be unnecessary. To remind the reader, the procedure was briefly as follows. All animals ran from the start box to a mid-box on every trial, and then to an end box, where they were rewarded on every trial. The 100 per cent reward group was also rewarded on every trial in the mid-box. The zero per cent reward group was never rewarded in the mid-box but was simply delayed there for a time equal to the time spent eating by the other group.

After the acquisition period was finished, the procedure of the present experiment diverged somewhat from that of the previous study. The difference stemmed from our attempt to make the animals relatively uninterested in food during the extinction trials. After the last acquisition trial a plentiful supply of dry pellets was put into the cage of each animal, and thereafter in the experiment, food was always present in the home cage. In addition, the animals were not run on the next two days to make sure that, before extinction began, they would get off the hunger rhythm to which they had become accustomed and would recover much of the weight they had lost.

Also, during the two days on which the animals were not run in the apparatus, an attempt was made to communicate to them that food was no longer available in the end box. Specifically, on each of these days each animal was put into the end box four different times and allowed to remain there without food for one minute. One may assume that this kind of procedure is at least somewhat effective in communicating to rats that food is no longer available: experiments on so-called "latent extinction" (Kimble, 1961, pp. 320–23) have shown that this kind of treatment does result in more rapid extinction. To the extent, then, that this procedure was effective, it indicated to the animals in the zero reward group that food was no longer available in the apparatus, and, to the 100 per cent reward group, that food was no longer available at least in the end box. To summarize: by the time the extinction trials were begun each animal had had two days during which food was always available in its home cage and had also had eight one-minute placements in the end box with no food there. We thus hoped that during the extinction trials the animals would have relatively little motivation for food in the experimental apparatus.

Just as in the preceding experiment, extinction trials were run from the start box to the mid-box. After a period of 20 seconds in the mid-box the animal was removed to its home cage. Three trials were run on each day. If an animal did not enter the mid-box in 120 seconds, it was removed from the runway. All animals were run on every trial regardless of how many times they refused to enter the mid-box. After 60 trials of extinction the experiment was discontinued. Fourteen animals were run in each of the two conditions in the experiment.

As one would expect, there was a difference in running times between the two groups of animals at the end of the acquisition period. The zero reward group ran much more slowly than the 100 per cent reward group. The mean running times at this point in the experiment are almost identical with the comparable figures for the experiment reported in Chapter 5. The 100 per cent reward group had an average running time of 1.8 seconds whereas in the previous experiment it was 1.9 seconds. The comparable figures for the zero reward groups are 4.6 seconds in this experiment and 4.2 seconds in the preceding one. This similarity of the figures between the two experiments is, of course, expected since the procedure during acquisition was identical. Nevertheless, it is comforting to have data showing that the identical procedure did indeed produce comparable results.

Let us now turn our attention to the data obtained during extinction, which are presented in Figure 6.1. The average running times during extinction, even on the first few trials, are not at all comparable to the times at the end of acquisition. This is, of course, to be expected, since the animals were hungry during acquisition and were not at all hungry during extinction. Consequently, both groups run much more slowly at the beginning of extinction. Consistent with the direction of the dif-

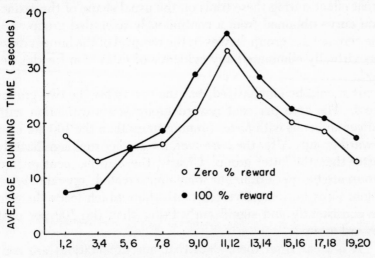

PAIRS OF DAYS DURING EXTINCTION (3 TRIALS PER DAY)

FIG. 6.1.—EXTINCTION UNDER LOW MOTIVATION (EXPERIMENT 9)

ference in running speeds at the end of acquisition, the 100 per cent reward group runs much faster than the zero reward group on these initial test trials. The figures are 7.6 seconds and 17.8 seconds, respectively, for the average on the first two days of extinction. This difference is significant at the .01 level of significance.

Thereafter, however, the course of events is interesting. As the figure shows, the 100 per cent reward group has the usual curve of extinction for the first 10 or 12 days. Its average running speed becomes slower and slower. The zero reward group, however, shows a most unusual effect. On the third and fourth days it actually runs somewhat faster than it did on the first two days, although not significantly so. The important point is that there is no evidence of any slowing down for the first eight days. On the ninth and tenth days these animals are still running almost as fast as they were on the first two days. By the tenth day the zero reward group is running faster than the 100 per cent reward group, a difference significant at the .06 level. In other words, for the first 30 extinction trials, the difference in performance between the two groups is noticeably marked. Removing the drive for food does not seem to have had any great effect during these trials on the usual shape of the extinction curve obtained from a continuously rewarded group. For the zero reward group, however, the removal of the hunger drive has virtually eliminated any evidence of extinction for this period.

It should be emphasized that the curves for the two groups cross. The zero per cent reward group starts extinction with slower and ends with *faster* running times than the 100 per cent reward group. After the crossover, the former runs significantly faster than the latter group. Clearly, the zero per cent reward group are not performing at some unmotivated "operant" level. There must be some directed motivation which leads them to be consistently and significantly faster than the 100 per cent reward group.

It is clear from these data that our expectations are confirmed. Animals trained under a zero reward schedule persist longer than continuously rewarded ones even though both are extinguished under conditions of minimal motivation. We seem to be justified in concluding that extra attractions continue to operate in the absence of the motivation that was dominant during training.

The evidence for the possibility that the zero reward group would show little if any indication of extinction is more complicated. During the first 24 trials these animals show a relatively weak but consistent willingness to run. There is no evidence of an extinction process for them during this period. All of this looks quite favorable to our supposition. But then, unfortunately, the next 12 trials provide clear evidence of decreased willingness to run. This should be decisive, except for the queer behavior shown in Figure 6.1 from the thirteenth day on. The zero reward group begins to run faster each day, until by the twentieth day its average running time is shorter than on the first day of extinction. This phenomenon is clearly much more than we bargained for, but obviously it invites speculation concerning dissonance reduction processes during extinction. Before indulging in speculation of this nature, however, the better part of valor indicates that we should try to replicate this outcome. This is especially necessary when it is observed that the continuously rewarded animals show the same increase in willingness to run, a result that we had no reason to expect.

*Experiment 10.—Comparison of Zero and Continuous Reward Groups: A Replication of Experiment 9*

The training conditions in this study were in every way identical to those described in the previous experiment. There were 12 animals in each group. The same apparatus, the same drive level, the same trial spacing, and the same number of trials were used. Again, both the 100 per cent and the zero reward groups found food in the end box on each trial, but whereas the 100 per cent reward group also found food on each trial in the mid-box the zero per cent reward group was simply detained there. Again, in the two days between acquisition and extinction, the animals had food always available and were given eight "latent extinction" trials in the end box.

On the last day of acquisition, the average running time for the 100 per cent reward animals was 1.7 seconds and for the zero per cent reward animals, 4.4 seconds. These times are strictly comparable to those obtained in Experiments 7 and 9. The results of the extinction trials for this replication are shown in Figure 6.2. Here the average running times are again plotted for blocks of six trials or two days.

The most obvious result is that, again, zero per cent reward animals tend to persist longer during extinction than the 100 per cent reward animals. They start out more slowly than the 100 per cent reward group, but on the last few days of extinction run faster than the other group. These differences, although not statistically so significant as those in Experiment 9, clearly support the findings of the previous study. Also, as in the previous experiment, the 100 per cent reward group shows an extinction curve. There is a progressive slowing up throughout the 60 trials. The curve of the zero per cent reward group, however, is rather distinctive: despite wide and unexplained daily variability, there is, for the zero reward group, no apparent progressive trend in the running times. Instead these animals, with the exception of days 5 and 6, maintain a fairly uniform running time throughout the 20 days of extinction.

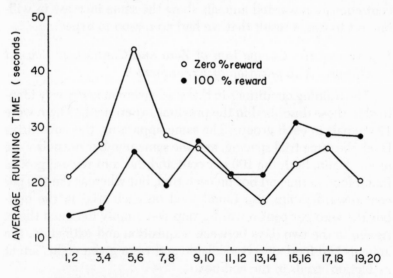

PAIRS OF DAYS DURING EXTINCTION (3 TRIALS PER DAY)

FIG. 6.2.—EXTINCTION UNDER LOW MOTIVATION (EXPERIMENT 10)

This behavior was also characteristic of the zero reward animals in the previous experiment, at least during the initial stages of extinction. In that experiment, these animals slowed down somewhat, but this was followed by subsequent improvement in running speed so that, at the end of extinction, they were running just as fast as before. In retrospect, one is tempted to interpret the peak at days 11 and 12 in Figure 6.1 as the same type of variability in daily performance that is obvious in the present experiment.

Since our procedure was identical for the two experiments, perhaps the best picture of the results may be obtained by combining the data, as shown in Figure 6.3. It seems clear that the 100 per cent reward group does, and the zero reward group does not, show evidence of extinction.

There is, then, evidence to support the following suggestions. Animals that have low motivation during extinction experience little dissonance during such trials. The failure to find food no longer has any real importance for them. At the same time, for animals that have previously experienced and reduced dissonance, subordinate motivations are still active so that the

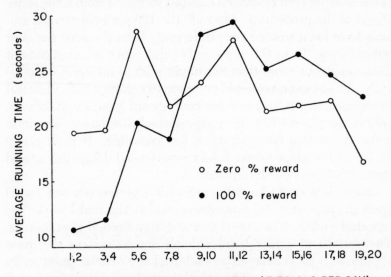

FIG. 6.3.—COMBINED RESULTS FOR EXTINCTION UNDER LOW MOTIVATION (EXPERIMENTS 9 AND 10)

extra attractions in the situation provide some justification for running. As long as these attractions remain stable, the animals show a weak but continued willingness to perform.

## Further Evidence for the Development of Extra Attractions

The procedures and results of the series of experiments presented earlier in this chapter suggested to us a way of designing a study that could more effectively support our theory concerning the development of extra attractions. These previous studies, which contrasted 100 per cent reward groups with zero per cent reward ones, provide some evidence that the extra attractions developed through dissonance reduction are associated, at least in part, with the place where dissonance was experienced. Of course, we assume that such attractions have also developed with respect to the activity involved and other aspects of the apparatus as well. But the results obtained when extinction trials were run from the start box to the mid-box imply that a considerable part of these attractions is concentrated in the area of the mid-box.

There is always the possibility, however, that the superiority of the zero per cent rewarded mid-box stemmed from some other aspect of the procedure. After all, the 100 per cent reward animals have been treated very differently from the zero per cent reward ones. To us this represents a difference in magnitude of dissonance, but other theorists might wish to interpret it differently. If, however, we could compare two groups with identical experience, that is, two zero per cent reward groups that differed only in the place where they experienced dissonance, we could make alternative interpretations less plausible. If each group preferred the place where it had experienced delay, this would strongly support our interpretation.

Such data could be collected with a preference test based upon the experimental procedures used in the mid-box studies reported earlier. The experimental design needed is as follows. Two groups of zero reward animals are trained in the same apparatus. One is delayed on each trial at a definite point on its route to the goal box. The other is similarly delayed on each trial, but at a distinctively different point in the apparatus. Each group should experience the same magnitude of dissonance and dissonance reduction as the result of the delay, but the extra attractions that develop should be largely associated with the stimuli characteristic of the delay place. Consequently, if the two groups are then given an opportunity to choose between these two delay places, each should show a preference for the one at which it had been delayed. Remembering our findings with conditions of low motivation during extinction, we thought these preferences would be somewhat more striking if the test trials were run with minimal motivation. Consequently, we designed and ran a new study.

*Experiment 11.—A Comparison of Two Zero Reward Groups*

The apparatus employed consisted of three runways, an end box, and two distinctive delay chambers. The first runway, painted gray, was 30 inches long. It led to the first delay chamber, which was 12 inches long, 12 inches wide, and 5 inches deep; it, too, was painted gray. There were guillotine doors at both the entrance and exit. This exit opened into a second runway, 48 inches long, painted white; it contained three evenly spaced hurdles, 3 inches high. This runway, in turn, opened into a second delay chamber. This was an unpainted box, 12 inches wide, 14 inches long, and 21 inches high, with an exit at the right rear corner. There were guillotine doors at both the entrance and exit. The exit opened into the third runway, at right angles to the second runway, which was 46 inches long and painted black. The last 10 inches formed the end box.

After taming and several days on a hunger schedule during which they had food available for two hours a day, the animals were given experience eating wet mash pellets in the goal box. They were then given 12 rewarded runs through the apparatus with all doors open. During the last 6 of these the hurdles were introduced and gradually increased in height to 3 inches. This preliminary training was spread over 6 days.

The animals were divided into two groups of 15 each. For the next 18 days both groups were run 4 trials a day with at least 30 minutes between trials. The only difference in procedure for the two groups was as follows. Delay Group 1 was delayed in the first delay chamber. At the time these animals entered it from the first runway, the exit gate was closed. The entrance door was closed after them. After a prescribed delay period the exit door was opened. These animals were never delayed in the second delay chamber. The animals in Delay Group 2, on the other hand, were never delayed in the first delay chamber, but they were held in the second delay chamber for an equal length of time before being released. During the first 10 training trials, this delay interval was gradually increased from 2 to 20 seconds and was kept at 20 seconds thereafter. All animals were rewarded on each trial with a wet mash pellet in the end box. One animal in Delay Group 1 died during training.

At the end of training, an ample supply of dry pellets was given each animal and thereafter food was continuously available. During the next 2 days, the animals were not run. Instead, each day they were placed in the end box without reward for four one-minute periods. Thus, at the beginning of extinction, all animals were under low food motivation and had had "latent extinction" experiences in the apparatus.

Extinction trials were then started and were given at the rate of 3 a day, with at least 30 minutes between trials. On these trials, the animal was placed directly in the first delay chamber, the exit door was then opened, and it was permitted to run the second alley and enter the second delay chamber. If it did so, the animal was retained there for 20 seconds and then returned to its home cage. If, instead, the animal retraced, and re-entered the first delay chamber, it was retained there for 20 seconds and then removed from the apparatus. If an animal did not enter the second delay chamber, or had not retraced to the first one, within 120 seconds, it was removed from the apparatus. Each animal was run on every trial. Clearly, the procedure we employed here was an attempt to combine a preference test between the two delay boxes and an extinction test in which we could record running speeds. This naturally introduces some problems with which we shall have to cope as they come up in presenting the results. This procedure of permitting the animals to return to the first delay box was maintained for 10 days, that is, 30 trials. The procedure was then changed to resemble usual extinction trials more closely. For another 10 days extinction trials were run from the first to the second delay box without permitting retracing. After the animals left the first delay box (which was the start box during extinction) the door was closed and they were not permitted to return to it.

Let us first look at the data relating to preferences between the two delay boxes. Group 1, it will be recalled, was delayed in the first delay box, and Group 2 was delayed in the second. If each of these groups has now developed some attractions in the place where it was delayed, we should expect a higher incidence of return to the first delay box by the animals of Group 1. The first two days of extinction show almost no returns to the first delay box by either group of animals. Undoubtedly, it took these 6 trials for the animals to comprehend the new situation, to understand that they were allowed to go to the second delay box and no farther. Starting on the third day of extinction the two groups show differential numbers of returns to the first delay box. On the fourth and fifth days of testing, the difference between the two groups is large and significant. On these two days, 10 of the 14 animals in Group 1 retrace at least once. Only 4 of the 15 animals in Group 2 do so. This difference yields a Chi-Square of 5.65, which is significant at the .02 level. The same difference can be seen in the average number of retracings. The animals in Group 2 show an average of only 0.4 returns to the first delay box on these two days, while the animals in Group 1 show an average of 1.2 returns to the place where this group had been delayed during training. Clearly, the animals that were delayed in Delay Box 1 did indeed prefer Delay Box 1 more than the animals that were delayed in Delay Box 2.

After the fifth day, the difference between the two groups had diminished, and by the tenth day it had disappeared altogether. During these latter days the number of returns for the animals that were delayed in Delay Box 2 increased, as if they were learning that a trial could be terminated by such behavior. Consequently, on the eleventh day we changed the procedure so as to prevent returns and ran the remainder of the trials as a simple extinction test.

The data comparing the two groups on running times are

presented in Figure 6.4. These data are presented only for days 1 and 2, on which there were very few returns to the starting delay box (three for Group 1 and four for Group 2), and for days 11 through 20, on which returns were not permitted.

On the first two days of extinction, both groups of animals run rather slowly, undoubtedly because of the removal of the hunger drive and also because of the unfamiliarity of the new procedure. Never before had either of the groups of animals been placed directly in Delay Box 1 to start a trial. On the first two days of extinction there is a large difference between the two groups, which is significant at the .05 level. Group 1, which was delayed in Delay Box 1, has an average of 28.0 seconds per trial, but Group 2, which was delayed in Delay Box 2, runs more slowly, with an average of 38.6 seconds per trial. This initial difference can be attributed to two factors. First of all, it reflects differences in speed of running the alley between the two delay boxes during acquisition. The group delayed in Delay Box 1

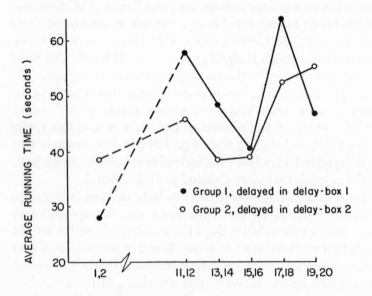

PAIRS OF DAYS DURING EXTINCTION (3 TRIALS PER DAY)

FIG. 6.4.—COMPARISON OF TWO DELAY GROUPS DURING EXTINCTION (EXPERIMENT 11)

ran this alley quickly and unhesitatingly, whereas the animals
in the other group showed noticeable hesitations in the alley
before entering Delay Box 2, where they were to experience
delay. The other factor that probably contributes to this initial
difference between the groups lies in their previous experience.
Group 1, although it had never been placed directly in Delay
Box 1 to start a trial, had had the experience of waiting there
until the door opened and then running on. Group 2, on the
other hand, had never had such experience. These animals had
always run directly through Delay Box 1. At any rate, these
initial differences exist. On days 11 and 12 it is clear that the
difference in running times between the two conditions has reversed itself. On days 11 through 14, Group 1 runs significantly
faster than Group 2 ( .10 level). After the fourteenth day of
extinction the difference between the two groups disappears.
It is unfortunate in some ways that we did not run all 60 trials
as a normal extinction procedure, since it is impossible to know
how the last 30 trials were affected by the experiences of having
been able to return to the starting delay box. However, it is also
valuable to have the preference data that we obtained at the
beginning of the testing.

All in all, taking the choice data and the data on time of
running, it seems justified to conclude that our expectations have
been supported. Although the effects are weak, there does seem
to be a tendency for Group 1 to prefer Delay Box 1 and for
Group 2 to prefer Delay Box 2. Group 1 is, at least, more willing
to return to Delay Box 1 and Group 2 runs more quickly to
Delay Box 2. We may say, then, that we have presented evidence that at least some of the dissonance which the animals
experience during delay is reduced by developing attraction for
the specific place where they were delayed.

### New Learning Based on Extra Attractions

Despite the weak effects observed in the above experiment,
we were optimistic enough to hope that these extra attractions
would be demonstrable in a test involving new learning. It was
hoped that once these extra attractions had become associated
with a given aspect of the situation, the lure of these would be

sufficiently strong to induce the animal to learn entirely new behaviors. We therefore designed and carried out two such studies, which are reported below. To anticipate, we had no difficulty in obtaining clear-cut evidence of learning when the only incentive was the opportunity to return to the place where dissonance reduction had occurred. The great ambiguity in each of the studies is that this learning is equally strong in both of our comparison groups.

## Experiment 12.—Extra Attractions as an Incentive for Lever Pressing

Two groups of 15 animals each were trained on the single mid-box apparatus that was described in Experiment 9. One group was trained on a zero reward schedule—it was only delayed and never rewarded in the mid-box. The other was on a 100 per cent reward schedule with food available in the mid-box on each trial. The training procedure was exactly as described in Experiment 9, that is, the same apparatus, the same number of trials, the same spacing, and so on. These animals also were given two days of ad lib feeding before the test trials began; they each had eight one-minute "latent extinction" experiences in the end box during this period; and all continued on ad lib feeding during the test trials.

For the test trials, the mid-box was removed from the training apparatus. A totally new start box was placed immediately before the entrance to the mid-box. At the front end of this start box was a metal pedal, one inch square, and one inch from the floor. When this was pressed, the door to the mid-box opened so that the animal could enter.

The procedure used in this new learning situation was as follows. The animal was placed in the start box and remained there until it had either pressed the pedal and entered the mid-box or until 3 minutes had passed. If it entered the mid-box, the door was closed and the animal was detained there for 20 seconds. If it had not pressed, or had pressed but not entered, it was removed from the apparatus after 3 minutes. Two trials a day were given, spaced approximately 30 minutes apart. Testing was continued for 20 days.

Our expectation, of course, was that both groups would show

some initial learning of the pedal-pushing response, the 100 per cent reward group because of secondary reward and the zero per cent reward group because of the extra attractions that had developed in the mid-box. We anticipated that the 100 per cent reward group would, however, show the rapid extinction that is usually the result when learning is based solely on secondary reward. We expected the zero per cent reward group, on the other hand, to learn and maintain its performance, assuming that the extra attractions would be enduring and intrinsic to the situation. This should be especially true when the animal has no strong interfering drive such as hunger. What actually occurred, however, was somewhat different.

On the first day, both groups took an average of about 50 seconds to press the pedal and enter the mid-box. During the next 7 days, both groups showed continual improvement to the point where their averages were between 12 and 15 seconds. For the remaining 12 days of testing, they each maintained this level, with only minor daily fluctuations and no indication of extinction. There was never any real difference in the performance of the two groups during the entire testing period.

We can assert with considerable assurance that the improvement in performance observed in this test was "real" learning. Taken alone, the behavior of the zero per cent reward group makes a good case for the presence of extra attractions in the situation. But the 100 per cent reward animals learn equally well. Perhaps secondary reward was effective for this latter group; perhaps, also, the particular task of pressing a lever to open a door has some intrinsic interest for the white rat. Myers and Miller (1954) and Seward and Procter (1960) present data compatible with this possibility. At any rate, the only legitimate conclusion that we can reach is that rats display very unusual behavior in this situation when they are satiated after a period of alley running.

## Experiment 13.—Extra Attractions as an Incentive for Maze Learning

In the hope of obtaining a demonstration of new learning based on the extra attractions due to dissonance reduction which would not be complicated by either of the above problems, we designed and carried out a second study. Two groups of 15 animals each were trained on the same apparatus and with the same procedure as that used in Experiment 11, the double delay box experiment. Just as before, one group experienced an unrewarded delay in the first delay box and the other in the second delay box. Thus, neither of these delay boxes should have acquired any secondary reward value. On the other hand, as the results of Experiment 11 showed, each of them had acquired some weak extra attractions for the group delayed in it.

For a new learning task, we constructed a four-unit U-maze. After two days of ad lib feeding and "latent extinction" experiences, both groups were run on the maze, using Delay Box 1 as the start box and Delay Box 2 as the end box. Our reasoning was that the group that had been delayed in Delay Box 2, which was now the end box, would have an incentive for running and learning the maze. The other group, however, which had been delayed in Delay Box 1 (which was now the start box), would not. If anything, this latter group would have some incentive for staying in the vicinity of the start box. All animals were given 2 trials a day, spaced approximately 30 minutes apart, for a period of 20 days. Retracing was permitted. Time and error scores were recorded. Each animal was allowed a 3-minute interval to traverse the maze and enter the end box. If it had not done so in this period, it was removed from the apparatus.

The results of this experiment are very similar to the results of the previous one in spite of the fact that secondary reward considerations are absent and a quite different task was used. Both groups, although not hungry and never obtaining food, show clear evidence of learning. Indeed, the learning is fairly rapid, but there is no evidence of any difference between the two groups. The evidence for the rapidity with which learning occurred can be seen in Figure 6.5, which presents, for the first 10 days of learning the maze (2 trials a day), the per cent of runs that were errorless or showed only one error. Naturally, this percentage is almost zero on the first day. The "chance level" indicated in Figure 6.5 is computed as though the animal ran the maze without any retracing. Clearly, with retracing permitted, the animals start below this "chance level." The curve then rises, until by the sixth day it has reached about 75 per cent

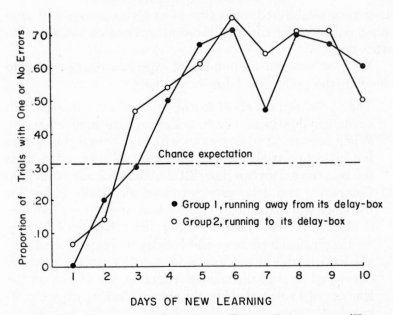

FIG. 6.5.–LEARNING A MAZE AFTER DELAY EXPERIENCES (EXPERI-MENT 13)

for each of the groups. Certainly, learning has occurred and the animals perform significantly better than "chance." There is, however, no consistent or significant difference between the two groups. The same pattern of clear learning with no difference between the two groups exists with respect to running times.

We again have good evidence of learning in non-hungry animals, even when no intrinsic reward is present. It is clear that the outcome of this study in no way supports our assumption of differentially located extra attractions for the two groups. Although we did find evidence that such attractions exist in this situation using extinction data, we find no such evidence in a new learning situation. It is possible that these extra attractions have been totally confounded with other types of incentive, possibly of the sort that Anderson (1941) describes under the concept of externalized motivation.

## Summary

We began this chapter with the suggestion that, according to the implications of dissonance theory, once extra attractions have been established, reduction of motivation should, if anything, enhance the effect of these attractions on resistance to extinction.

We have presented a number of experiments attempting to elucidate this point. We have shown that:

1. The partial reward effect is still obtained even though both training and extinction occur under very low motivation.
2. When acquisition trials are run with high hunger motivation but extinction trials are run with minimal motivation, zero per cent reward groups show little evidence of any extinction.
3. Comparing two delay groups treated identically except for the place where the delay occurred, we were able to demonstrate with low motivation testing that preferences develop for the particular place in which delay was experienced.
4. We were unable to produce evidence that extra attractions, developed through dissonance reduction, would support the learning of a new task when the animal is otherwise not motivated.

# 7

# Effort, Expectation, and Amount
# of Reward

Thus far our discussion, and the experimental evidence, have
been concerned almost exclusively with the effects of partial reward and delay of reward. It will be recalled from Chapter 2
that, according to our theoretical explanation, increased effort
expenditure would be expected to have the same kinds of effects.
That is, the more effort an animal is required to exert during
training, the more resistant to extinction should the animal be.
The information that the animal has concerning the expenditure
of energy and effort is dissonant with continuing to engage in
the action in the same way that information concerning absence
of reward, or information concerning delay, is dissonant with
continuing. The greater the effort required, the greater would
be the magnitude of dissonance, and, hence, the greater the development of extra attraction for something in the situation in
order to reduce dissonance. Thus, greater effort requirement
would result in greater resistance to extinction.

*The Direct Effect of Effort*

It will be recalled from Chapter 1 that the existing evidence
supports this implication of the theory. In general, the existing
data can be summarized by saying that, if conditions during extinction are held constant, then the more effort that is required
of the animal during acquisition, the greater is its resistance to
extinction. This is reassuring data, in a sense, but a procedure
that involves differential changes for various groups between

acquisition and extinction inevitably results in some ambiguity of interpretation. It is always possible to explain the results from such experiments on the basis of decrements or increments of behavior resulting from changed stimulus conditions, rather than on the basis of extra attractions that have developed in reducing dissonance introduced by effort. Consequently, it would be valuable to demonstrate that increased effort during training results in increased resistance to extinction in 100 per cent rewarded animals even if conditions are not changed at all between training and extinction trials. Clearly, in order to produce such results one would need a situation where, for the high effort condition, the extra attractions that had developed would be more powerful than the discouragement of running during extinction owing to the larger expenditure of energy needed.

We proceeded to attempt such a demonstration. In order to do this we arbitrarily selected an activity in which the expenditure of effort by the animal could be varied experimentally and which, intuitively, seemed not to represent too strong a deterrent to action. The apparatus selected was a runway that could be inclined at varying angles. Clearly, the steeper the slope, the more effort would be required and the more dissonance introduced on each trial. The first experiment was a preliminary one to explore the adequacy of the situation for our purposes. One group of animals ran a level runway during acquisition; another group ran the runway at an angle of 45 degrees; and a third group had variable experience—that is, on some trials the runway was level and on other trials it was tilted 45 degrees. This last group was run because of the possibility that such variable experience might increase the magnitude of the effects we were looking for: it seemed possible that high effort might introduce more dissonance for an animal if it had a comparison with experiences in which it obtained the same reward with considerably less effort. The animals were extinguished under conditions paralleling the acquisition conditions. The "level group" was extinguished on a level runway; the "45 degree group" and the "variable 45 degree group" were both extinguished on a 45 degree runway.

The data were encouraging: The "level group" extinguished

most quickly, the "45 degree group" next, and the "variable 45 degree group" least quickly. The differences, however, tended to be slight, and because of the few animals employed and changes in procedure which we felt were justified in a preliminary experiment, no great faith can be placed in the results. Consequently, we do not report the experimental procedure or the results in any detail. We were sufficiently encouraged, however, to conduct another, more adequate experiment.

*Experiment 14.—The Effect of Effort on Extinction with 100 Per Cent Reward*

The apparatus for the experiment was a 7-foot enclosed runway which could be adjusted to inclines of 0, 25, or 50 degrees. A start box and a goal box were hinged to the runway in such a way that they would remain level whatever the inclination of the runway. Sixty-four naïve albino rats, 32 males and 32 females, were used, all of them between 89 and 104 days old at the start of the experiment. Two animals died during the course of the experiment. After being tamed, the animals were put on a 22-hour food-deprivation schedule and were adapted to eating food pellets in the goal box. They were then divided into two equal groups, the 25 degree incline group and the 50 degree incline group. During the next 5 days, each group was given 8 rewarded trials of running the alley set at the appropriate incline.

The animals of each incline group were then divided into two equal subgroups. One subgroup (invariable effort) continued to receive all its trials (5 a day) at the appropriate incline. The other subgroup (variable effort) received 3 of the 5 daily trials at its appropriate incline and the other 2 trials with the runway level. This training continued for 12 days, a total of 60 training trials. Trials were spaced at least 8 minutes apart.

Extinction trials were run for the next 11 days, 5 spaced trials a day as during training. All the 50 degree animals, that is, both the invariable and variable subgroups, were extinguished on the 50 degree slope. All the 25 degree animals were extinguished on the 25 degree slope. No level runway trials were given during extinction. If an animal failed to enter the goal box within

90 seconds after the start door had been raised, it was removed from the apparatus. After an animal accumulated four 90-second trials, not necessarily consecutive, it was considered extinguished and was not run any more.

The differences in resistance to extinction between the variable and invariable effort subgroups, although in the same direction as for the preliminary experiment, were very slight and not significant. For analysis and presentation of the data, therefore, we have combined the variable and invariable subgroups, so as to compare the low effort group (25 degree incline) with the high effort group (50 degree incline). Since the differences that were found between the high and low effort groups occurred under both variable and invariable training conditions, throwing the data together for ease of presentation seems justified.

Table 7.1 presents the data for the average number of trials to reach the criterion of four 90-second trials during extinction. The low effort group reaches this criterion in an average of 20.6 trials, whereas the high effort group takes 28.3 trials, a difference significant at the .01 level. It should be remembered that this difference exists even though the conditions during extinction favor the low effort group, that is, for each group conditions during extinction are the same as conditions during acquisition.

The same differences are reflected in running times during extinction. Table 7.2 presents these data. There is no appreciable difference in running times between the two groups on the last day of acquisition. The difference that does exist, as one might expect, slightly favors the low effort group, which has less work to do and consequently runs slightly faster. During extinction, however, the two effort conditions quickly diverge. During the first 5 trials on the first day of extinction the low effort group already begins to slow up relative to the high effort

TABLE 7.1

AVERAGE NUMBER OF TRIALS TO EXTINCTION
(EXPERIMENT 14)

| Incline Group | N | Number of Trials to Extinction |
|---|---|---|
| 25 degree | 31 | 20.6 |
| 50 degree | 31 | 28.3 |

TABLE 7.2

Average Running Time on Extinction (in Seconds)
for Different Effort Conditions (Experiment 14)

| | Effort Condition | |
|---|---|---|
| | 25° Incline (N = 31) | 50° Incline (N = 31) |
| Last day of acquisition | 1.8 | 2.0 |
| First day of extinction | 7.1 | 3.8 |
| Second day of extinction | 26.1 | 16.4 |
| Third day of extinction | 37.2 | 31.0 |

group. This difference between the two groups persists. In short, this is a situation where the extra attraction built up during acquisition is sufficient to more than compensate for the differential effort during extinction. We thus have more evidence to support the theoretical implications about the relationship between effort expenditure and magnitude of dissonance.

*Effort and Partial Reward*

Granted, then, that effort does introduce dissonance and increases resistance to extinction, it seems plausible to suppose that, when added to a partial reward situation, increased effort would augment the partial reward effect. It was, of course, these considerations which influenced the design of Experiment 5, reported in Chapter 4. It will be recalled that the activity required of the animals in that experiment was very effortful. The rats were required to jump over two rather high hurdles and to push under three rather heavily weighted doors in order to go from the start box to the food compartment. It will also be recalled that, from Experiment 5, we obtained data showing that resistance to extinction was a simple function of the absolute number of times the animal experienced unrewarded trials and was *not* a function of the ratio of reward during training.

After that experiment had been completed, it occurred to us that it would be valuable to have a precise comparison between high and low effort conditions for these data. We therefore repeated the experiment as exactly as we could, but with little effort required of the animal.

*Experiment 15.—Cumulative Effects of Partial Reward with
    Low Effort*

In this low effort version of Experiment 5 the hurdles were
entirely removed from the apparatus and the doors were counterbalanced to open with the slightest pressure from the animal
and to remain open after the animal pushed through. In this
way, the activity was kept much the same as that required in
Experiment 5, but the degree of physical effort the animal had
to expend was considerably reduced. Otherwise, the procedure
was identical to that in the high effort experiment. In order to
make the two experiments as comparable as possible in all details other than effort, exactly the same number of preliminary
training trials was given and exactly the same pattern of reward
and non-reward was used throughout.

Only four of the eleven experimental conditions from the
high effort experiment were repeated using low effort. One 50
per cent reward group was run for 16 unrewarded trials, and another 50 per cent reward group was run for 72 unrewarded trials.
Because the high effort experiment had shown the ratio of reward to be quite unimportant, we thought that these two partial
reward groups would suffice for a comparison with the high
effort experiment. The other two conditions that we repeated
using low effort were both conditions of 100 per cent reward.
One of these groups was run for zero additional trials after preliminary training and the other for 54 additional trials.

The attempt to compare high and low effort conditions in
this experiment faces some methodological problems. If the two
groups that were trained with different effort requirements were
both to be extinguished with constant effort, there would obviously be a gross change in the behavior required for at least one
of the groups. We wanted to avoid the ambiguities of interpretation resulting from such procedures and consequently chose
to extinguish both groups with the same effort conditions that
each had experienced during training.

This procedure, however, involved us in other, equally difficult problems. Certainly, in the low effort conditions, running
times would be faster during both acquisition and extinction.
The number of trials to a criterion of extinction would also be

greater for the low effort condition if the same criterion of extinction were to be used for both groups. Because of the obviously strong deterrent effect of a heavily weighted door, such a difference between the high and low effort groups would exist solely because of the effort required during extinction, regardless of training conditions. Thus, if the same criterion of extinction were used, conclusions concerning the effects of differential effort during acquisition might be almost impossible. In view of these problems, we decided to find two different criteria of extinction which would produce roughly comparable measures of resistance to extinction for the two effort groups. The two conditions of 100 per cent reward in the low effort experiment were intended to provide the basis on which we could judge the comparability of our measures of resistance to extinction. If we chose criteria of extinction that made the 100 per cent reward groups almost equal in resistance to extinction in the high and low effort experiments, then we might be safe in assuming that we had roughly comparable measures and could directly compare the partial reward groups in the two experiments.

It will be recalled that, in the high effort experiment, the criterion of extinction was six trials, not necessarily consecutive, on which the animal did not reach the food compartment in 180 seconds. On the basis of some preliminary exploration, and on the basis of hunch, intuition, and hope, we arbitrarily chose as the criterion of extinction in the low effort experiment, six trials, not necessarily consecutive, on which the animal did not reach the food compartment in 30 seconds. We proved to be reasonably fortunate in this choice of criterion since we did obtain rough comparability of measures for the 100 per cent reward groups.

The effects of effort on resistance to extinction after partial reward are shown in Table 7.3. This table presents the geometric mean number of trials to extinction for the four low effort groups and the comparable figures for the high effort experiment. It may be seen from examining the first two rows of figures that we did, fortunately, achieve rough comparability of measures of resistance to extinction. The two 100 per cent reward conditions in the low effort experiment have averages of

TABLE 7.3

AVERAGE TRIALS TO EXTINCTION FOR HIGH AND LOW
EFFORT CONDITIONS (EXPERIMENT 15)

| | Effort | |
| --- | --- | --- |
| | High | Low |
| 100 Per Cent Reward | 15.2 | 14.0 |
| (zero trials) | (N = 11) | (N = 13) |
| 100 Per Cent Reward | 19.8 | 17.7 |
| (54 trials) | (N = 14) | (N = 23) |
| Partial Reward | 27.6 | 30.6 |
| (16 unrewarded trials) | (N = 37) | (N = 23) |
| Partial Reward | 52.4 | 38.2 |
| (72 unrewarded trials) | (N = 40) | (N = 11) |

14.0 and 17.7 trials to the criterion of extinction. The comparable figures for the corresponding high effort conditions are 15.2 and 19.8. The differences between the two experiments for the 100 per cent reward conditions are very slight.

The last two rows of figures in the table give the data for the partial reward groups. It is clear that the difference between the high and low effort groups that experienced 16 unrewarded trials is negligible. The low effort group extinguishes in 30.6 trials and the high effort group in 27.6 trials. There is, however, a large difference between the two effort experiments for the animals that experienced 72 unrewarded trials. For both experiments, as the number of unrewarded trials increases, there is a marked increase in resistance to extinction. This increase is large for the high effort condition and considerably smaller for the low effort condition—a difference significant at the .02 level. We thus have some tentative support for the statement that additional physical effort, by increasing the magnitude of dissonance that is introduced on unrewarded trials, augments the effect of partial reward on resistance to extinction.

Although it is encouraging to have obtained such a difference between the high and low effort groups, one cannot ignore the difficulty of interpreting all the data. If the greater exertion of physical effort increases the magnitude of dissonance introduced on each unrewarded trial, then one would expect the effect to be discernible even after 16 unrewarded trials.

The difficulty lies in the essential non-comparability of our measures. In order to get some degree of comparability between the two experiments, we tried to, and were successful in, obtaining roughly equal resistance to extinction for the 100 per cent reward conditions. And it is only with respect to this base line that the two experiments show equal resistance to extinction after 16 unrewarded trials. But if one had measures of resistance to extinction that were really comparable, would we theoretically expect the 100 per cent reward conditions in the high and low effort experiments to be equal?

As we pointed out early in the chapter, it is impossible to answer this question generally. It depends on whether the extra attractions which have developed in the high effort condition are or are not sufficient to outweigh the greater deterrent effect of high effort during extinction. Because of this unclarity we really cannot directly compare the resistance to extinction of separate groups between the high and low effort condition. One is safe only in comparing the increment in resistance to extinction as the number of unrewarded trials increases. On this comparison, which is quite unambiguous, we have clear evidence supporting our theory.

Nevertheless, even though the results are favorable, the methodological problems left us somewhat unhappy, and we therefore performed an additional experiment in an attempt to obtain a comparison that would be methodologically more adequate.

*Experiment 16.—Partial Reward with and without*
*Physical Effort*

We attempted to solve the problem of comparability by an extension of the placing experiment (Experiment 6) that we reported in Chapter 4. It will be recalled that three groups were run in that experiment: (1) a 100 per cent reward group; (2) a 50 per cent reward group; and (3) a "placed" group, which had the same reward schedule as the 50 per cent reward group but was placed directly in the goal box on unrewarded trials. We found that the "placed" group did not show any greater resistance to extinction than did the 100 per cent group. Since this "placed" group had exactly the same pattern of rewards and non-rewards as the 50 per cent reward group, it is possible to view it as a condition demanding no effort on unrewarded trials. This "placed" group also discriminated between trials when it was placed in the goal box and not rewarded and trials when it had to run the alley; on placed trials, therefore, these animals had no expectation of any reward. Thus, the "placed" group differed from the partially rewarded group both in lack of effort and in lack of food expectation on unrewarded trials.

By adding a fourth group to such an experiment we could have a more definitive test of both the effect of expectation and the effect of physical effort. This fourth group would be a "partial placed" one. It would be treated similarly to the "placed" group: that is, every time the animals in the "partial placed" condition ran the runway, they would be rewarded. On trials that were unrewarded they would be placed directly in the goal box. But these animals would also be given some trials on which they were placed directly in the goal box and *were* rewarded. They would in this way maintain an expectation of reward and would look for food on those trials when they were placed directly in the goal box. There still would be a clear differential, however, between this group and the normal 50 per cent reward group in the amount of effort expended on unrewarded trials. Thus, this "partial placed" group, when compared with a usual partial reward group, would enable us to assess the effect of increased effort on resistance to extinction following partial reward. The comparison between the "partial placed" and "placed" groups would show the effect of expectation on unrewarded trials.

There is some evidence in the literature that such a partially placed group is definitely superior to a placed group and even somewhat superior to a group that is rewarded 100 per cent of the time. Lewis and Cotton (1958) report a study in which, after training on a black-white discrimination, all animals were given a series of massed placements in the "correct goal box." One group was rewarded on each placed trial, another group was never rewarded on any of the placed trials, and a third group was rewarded on 50 per cent of these trials. Following this placement procedure, extinction trials were run. The animals that had only unrewarded placements extinguished most quickly. The animals that had a 50 per cent reward schedule on the placements went back to the "correct goal box" significantly more often during extinction than those that had only rewarded placement trials. In other words, there is evidence that a "partial placed" group will be more resistant to extinction than either a "placed" group or a 100 per cent group. From these data, however, we do not know how a "partial placed" group would compare with a normal 50 per cent reward group. On the basis of dissonance theory we should expect the normal 50 per cent group that expends more effort to be more resistant to extinction.

The experiment that we ran was a replication of Experiment 6, with the addition of the "partial placed" group. This "partial placed" group was run exactly as the "placed" group, with one exception: on each day they were given an additional trial, randomly inserted among the other trials. On this additional trial they were placed directly in the food compartment, where they found food. In other words, the 100 per cent reward group ran the runway and found food six times a day; the 50 per cent reward group ran the runway six times a day, finding food three times in six trials; the "placed" group ran the runway three times a day, finding food each time, and were placed in the food compartment three times each day with no food available; the "partial placed" animals ran three trials each day, finding food on each trial, and were placed directly in the food compartment four times each day, finding food on one of these four placed trials. The acquisition trials lasted for 12 days. Following this, extinction trials were run (also six a day), all groups of animals being treated identically. If, during extinction, an animal did not reach the food compartment in 60 seconds, it was removed from the apparatus.

Table 7.4 presents, for these four groups, the average number of trials to reach a criterion of extinction (two trials, not necessarily consecutive, on which the animal failed to reach the food compartment in 60 seconds). The three groups that constituted a replication of Experiment 6 show confirming results. The 100 per cent reward condition has an average of 18.3 trials

TABLE 7.4

AVERAGE NUMBER OF TRIALS TO EXTINCTION
IN PLACING VS. RUNNING EXPERIMENT (EXPERIMENT 16)

| Training Condition | N | Mean Number of Trials to Extinction |
|---|---|---|
| 100 Per Cent Reward | 12 | 18.3 |
| 50 Per Cent Reward | 12 | 38.3 |
| "Partial Placed" | 12 | 30.5 |
| "Placed" | 10 | 15.4 |

to extinction, the "placed" group again shows slightly faster extinction, with an average of 15.4 trials, and the 50 per cent reward group is significantly (.01 level) more resistant to extinction than either of them, taking an average of 38.3 trials to reach the criterion.

The results for the "partial placed" group are of particular interest. They take 30.5 trials, on the average, to reach the extinction criterion. These "partial placed" animals are significantly (.01 level) more resistant to extinction than the 100 per cent reward animals or the "placed" animals. In other words, if one creates a situation in which the animal expects to find food, looks for it, and does not find it, one has introduced dissonance and thus increased the resistance to extinction, even though the amount of physical effort is very slight on these unrewarded trials. The "partial placed" animals, however, are significantly less resistant to extinction (.05 level) than the 50 per cent reward animals. This comparison, of course, gives a clear, unambiguous picture of the effect of effort itself. If, holding expectation constant, the amount of effort on the unrewarded trials is increased, the magnitude of dissonance introduced on these trials is greater, and the resistance to extinction is correspondingly greater.

It is also of interest to look at the running times during extinction for these four groups of animals. All animals were run for at least 30 trials, that is, for five days of extinction trials. Figure 7.1 presents the average running times by days of extinction for the first five days. It is clear that the differences we observed on number of trials to an extinction criterion are also present when we look at the running times. The running times

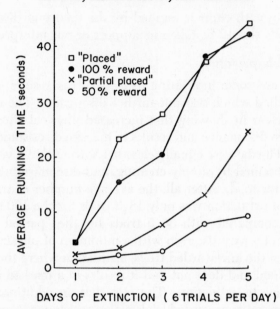

FIG. 7.1.—RESISTANCE TO EXTINCTION AFTER PLACING AND PARTIAL REWARD (EXPERIMENT 15)

for the last days of acquisition are not presented because all four groups were almost identical, averaging either 1.7 or 1.8 seconds.

The 100 per cent reward group and the "placed" group are very similar in their running times during extinction. The only difference is a slight one on the second and third days, during which the "placed" group was somewhat slower. The 50 per cent reward group and the "partial placed" group are both considerably faster during extinction than the other two groups. On the third day of extinction the curves of running times for the 50 per cent reward animals and the "partially placed" animals begin to diverge. The 50 per cent reward animals, which expended more effort on unrewarded trials, continue to run rather fast, while the "partial placed" animals, which expended less effort on unrewarded trials, begin slowing down very markedly on the fourth and fifth days. We can accept the assertion that increased effort during partial reward intensifies the effect of unrewarded experiences on resistance to extinction. Since this relationship with effort is implied by the theory of dissonance, these results should be taken in support of our interpretation.

## Effort and Expectation

There are some interesting aspects to the results we have just described which warrant further discussion. The data are certainly clear in showing that increased physical effort introduces more dissonance and results in increased resistance to extinction. The data are equally clear in showing that a very large effect is obtained by simply creating, and disconfirming, an expectation for food. After all, the average number of trials to a criterion of extinction was only 18.3 trials for the 100 per cent group as compared with 30.5 trials for the "partial placed" group. In other words, even with a minimum of physical effort required on the unrewarded trials, a situation where the animal looks for food and does not find it results in a marked increase in resistance to extinction. The fact that an additional effort requirement on unrewarded trials makes resistance to extinction even greater is, of course, of crucial theoretical interest to us, but it does not detract from the importance of the effect of simply not finding reward when the animal looks for it.

These data have important bearing on the explanations of partial reward effects which have been proposed by theorists such as Weinstock (1954) and Estes (1959). The fact that resistance to extinction is so markedly enhanced by the mere disconfirmation of an expectation, even when the animal does not perform the complete act of running the alley, presents a strong argument against any theoretical account of partial reward effects that relies on the concept of competing responses. These explanations demand that the failure to find food when it is expected should give rise to competing responses. Even more importantly, these competing responses should become anticipatory so that they occur while the animal is running the alley. In our "partial placed" group, however, this latter is very unlikely to have taken place. The disconfirmation of the expectancy never occurred on trials when the animal ran, only on placed trials. Thus there is every reason for the animal to make a distinction between the consequences to be expected on running and on placed trials, and little reason for competing responses to occur on the former. That this is true in our experiment is suggested by the fact that the running times of the "partial placed" and 100 per cent reward animals were strictly comparable throughout training. Granted, then, that such competing responses did not become anticipatory for the "partial placed" animals, there is no way in which "competing response" explanations could account for the increased resistance to extinction found for this group.

These data also lead us to some interesting implications concerning the effect of magnitude of reward on resistance to extinction. By now, it is undoubtedly clear to the reader what the theory of dissonance would have to say about variations in magnitude of reward. One obviously must consider the amount of reward in relation to the amount of effort required of the animal in order to assess the magnitude of dissonance that would be introduced on any given trial, even when the animal finds food on every trial. Certainly, it would be possible to find a situation where the effort required was high enough, and the amount of reward was low enough, so that each trial introduced appreciable dissonance. Holding the effort requirement constant, the smaller the amount of reward, the more dissonance would be introduced and the greater would be the resistance to extinction. One would therefore expect that with 100 per cent reward during training, less reward should be associated with greater resistance to extinction.

What, however, would we say about the effects of magnitude of reward on animals trained on a partial reward schedule? Under such circumstances, of course, the magnitude of dissonance introduced on unrewarded trials far outweighs the effects of effort on rewarded trials. We have seen that expecting and being oriented toward food is crucial on the unrewarded trials. It seems plausible, consequently, to expect that the larger the amount of food that the animal is accustomed to receiving as a reward, the greater will be the dissonance introduced on an unrewarded trial. Since a greater magnitude of dissonance will result in greater dissonance reduction through developing some extra attraction in the situation, we come to an interesting conclusion: with partial reward training, greater magnitude of reward should result in greater resistance to extinction.

An excellent experiment is reported in the literature which is directly pertinent to the above discussion. Hulse (1958) reports a study in which he varied percentage of reward and amount of reward. Four conditions that he reports are of interest to us: 100 per cent reward with 1.0 gram of food, 100 per cent reward with 0.08 gram, 46 per cent reward with 1.0 gram, and 46 per cent reward with 0.08 gram. There are, in other words, two conditions of 100 per cent reward, one receiving a relatively large amount of food and the other a very small amount, and two comparable conditions of partial reward.

The animals were run in a straight runway to food. Each animal was given only one trial a day. After preliminary training they were given 24 training trials. The partial reward groups thus had 13 unrewarded experiences. They were then given 19 extinction trials, again only one a day. Table 7.5 presents the mean running speeds for the four conditions mentioned above. There were 18 animals in each group.

TABLE 7.5

MEAN RUNNING SPEEDS DURING EXTINCTION
FOR FOUR CONDITIONS FROM EXPERIMENT BY HULSE (1958)

| Amount of Reward | Reward Schedule | |
|---|---|---|
| | 100% | 46% |
| 1.0 gram | 12.5 | 44.0 |
| 0.08 gram | 21.3 | 25.0 |

The results are rather striking. When trained on a 100 per cent reward schedule, the animals that received a very small reward were significantly more resistant to extinction than those that received a large reward. For animals trained on a partial reward schedule the reverse is true: the large reward group is significantly more resistant to extinction than the small reward group. We have confirmation, then, of two points: (1) too small a reward for 100 per cent animals may result in dissonance, and (2) greater dissonance is introduced on an unrewarded trial if the animal is accustomed to a large reward than if it is accustomed to a small reward.

*Summary*

We have presented and discussed experimental evidence related to three variables—effort, expectation of reward, and magnitude of reward. The following implications of our theory have been supported:

1. Increased effort results in greater resistance to extinction regardless of the reward schedule.
2. Even with minimal effort involved, the absence of reward when the animal is oriented toward obtaining reward increases its resistance to extinction.
3. The greater the magnitude of reward expected, the greater the dissonance introduced on an unrewarded trial and the greater the consonance on a rewarded trial. Thus, with 100 per cent reward, the larger reward decreases resistance to extinction, whereas with partial reward it increases resistance.

In addition, we have presented experimental evidence that casts doubt on "competing response" explanations of the partial reward effect.

# 8

# A Speculative Summary

We have presented a new explanation for a considerable body of empirical data. Specifically, we have applied the theory of dissonance to explain why partial reward, delay of reward, and effort expenditure during training result in increased resistance to extinction. We have tried to demonstrate that this theoretical explanation has validity. It can account for data with which other theories have difficulty, it integrates empirical phenomena that have been regarded as unrelated, and it is supported by the results of experiments designed specifically to test its implications.

When a new theoretical explanation is offered, however, one must look at it critically. Are there vaguenesses and ambiguities in the theoretical statement; do data exist that are not compatible with the theory; are there other more plausible and more parsimonious explanations of the same data? By way of summary, we shall take a critical look at the theory and the data, and, at the same time, indulge in some speculations concerning broader implications of the theory.

The bare skeleton of the theory, as applied here, can be summarized briefly: If an organism continues to engage in an activity while possessing information that, considered alone, would lead it to discontinue the activity, it will develop some extra attraction for the activity or its consequences in order to give itself additional justification for continuing to engage in the behavior. In rather loose terms, this is the entire statement of the theory. Clearly, in order to make any predictions from the theory and to have them be relevant to data, some flesh has to be put on this skeleton. Let us examine precisely how this is done, the problems that arise, and the problems that remain unsolved.

*How do we know when an organism possesses information that, considered alone, would lead it to discontinue an activity?*

One must, of course, specify on independent, a priori grounds when an organism can be said to possess information that is dissonant with continuing an activity. By definition, if an organism possessed only information dissonant with engaging in some activity, we would observe a cessation of the activity. But we are interested primarily in situations where the organism also has consonant information so that it *continues* to engage in the behavior in spite of the dissonance. In such a situation, however, one ought to be able to see some hesitation, some evidence of unwillingness to perform the action. Such hesitation might then be an indication of the existence of dissonance. Indeed, in situations which intuitively fit our theoretical requirements, such as partial reward and delay of reward situations, hesitation and longer running times are observed during acquisition trials.

There are difficulties, however, in relying on such a measure as an indication of the existence of dissonance, the major one being that this particular measure is obtained during the process (according to the theory) of the development of extra attractions. Would not the development of these extra attractions, if the theory is correct, interfere with the validity of such a measure as an indication of the existence of dissonance? The answer, of course, is yes. There are many indications in data in the literature that as training progresses, the difference in running speeds between, say, a partially rewarded group and a 100 per cent rewarded group tends to become less and less and ultimately to disappear; sometimes it even reverses its direction (Goodrich, 1959).

The solution that we offer to this problem is to propose that one test whether a variable produces such hesitation effects generally in a standardized test apparatus. One would have animals

run a simple runway for food. Any factor which, when introduced, slowed their running, would be said to represent information dissonant with running. We would of course find that
soon after the introduction of unrewarded trials, delay of reward, or increased effort the running would be slower. We thus
accept this test procedure as an operational measure of whether
or not a given factor provides the animal with information dissonant with continuing to engage in an activity. According to
the theory, any variable that produces hesitation in our test
apparatus will result in the development of extra attraction after
a reasonably prolonged series of trials, provided the animal does
not stop performing the action. It is necessary to point out that
this operational definition, although it sounds very precise and
specific, is not foolproof. There are things that could produce
hesitation in an animal that are not, we would all agree, deterrents to action. For example, the sudden introduction of some
new stimulus, like the sound of a buzzer, would undoubtedly
slow the animal down temporarily. How to distinguish such
factors from true deterrents without resorting to our intuition
is an unsolved problem. Perhaps the temporary nature of the
effects of the introduction of novel stimuli would provide a key
to making this distinction operationally.

Nonetheless, our operational specification enables the theory
to have some predictive power. It brings together, as psychologically identical, various operations that appear to be different. We have shown that partial reward, delay of reward, and
effort expenditure, all three of which are similar from the point
of view of dissonance theory, do indeed have similar effects in
prolonging resistance to extinction.

There is in the literature, however, a group of studies which,
at first sight, seems to contradict our theoretical interpretation.
At least one kind of situation has been studied in which partial
reward during training does not increase resistance to extinction, the crucial aspect of this situation being that the sequence
of rewards and non-rewards is patterned in certain special ways.
Thus it has been shown that if rewards and non-rewards alter-
nate, partial reward results in no greater resistance to extinction
than does 100 per cent reward (Tyler *et al.*, 1953; Capaldi,

1958). It has also been shown (Grosslight and Radlow, 1956, 1957) that if all the unrewarded trials occur only at the end of a day's runs, partial reward does not increase resistance to extinction.

This apparent contradiction with our theory can be dealt with rather easily. If the patterning of rewards and non-rewards is such that the animal can discriminate between trials that are to be rewarded and those that are not to be rewarded, then partial reward will not increase resistance to extinction. What happens, of course, is that the animal does not expect food on an unrewarded trial and so such a patterning fails to produce any dissonance. That is, when the animal does not expect food, not finding food does not introduce dissonance. As one might expect, when rewarded and unrewarded trials are alternated, running times on unrewarded trials are much longer than on rewarded trials. In short, if the animal does not expect food, it shows little eagerness to run and no dissonance is introduced.

The same kind of discrimination between rewarded and unrewarded trials undoubtedly occurs in the experiments in which unrewarded trials conclude the day's runs. As the animal gets close to the last trials of the day, it may stop expecting rewards and the unrewarded trial then may have a different significance. We hesitate to emphasize this explanation, however, because the studies that have been reported suffer from other difficulties also. They deal with discrimination and reversal learning under conditions where the initial discrimination is very inadequately learned. Inadequate learning may also have interfering effects.

There does exist one study that we are unable to explain to our own satisfaction. Wike *et al.* (1959) report a study using patterning of delay of reward and immediate reward. From our theory, we would not expect patterning to affect delay of reward in the same way that it affects partial reward. Even if the animal expects the delay, it should still introduce dissonance—indeed, if it did not, how would one account for the increased resistance to extinction resulting from delay on *every* acquisition trial?

This experiment by Wike *et al.* contains two parts. In one part a random mixture of delayed and immediate rewards is compared with an alternating sequence. As we should expect with delay of reward, the animals that experienced the alternating sequence are as resistant to extinction as the other group. In the other part of the study, the authors compare a group receiving no delays, a group receiving delay in the middle of a day's runs, and a group receiving delay at the end of a day's runs. We should, of course, expect both of the delay groups to be equally superior to the group that was always rewarded immediately. But this is not the case. On the contrary, the group that received delay only at the end of the day's runs was less resistant to extinction than the other delay group and about equal to the immediate reward group. This result is surprising to us and we have no ready explanation for it. Should it prove to be a replicable finding, it would mean that factors other than the ones with which we have dealt must also be taken into consideration.

All in all, the data on partial reward, delay of reward, and effort fit our theory well. But have we examined in detail other factors that also fit our operational definition? The answer is clearly no. There is at least one major gap in the data we have presented, namely, data on punishment. But these data should certainly not be ignored. If we inserted punishment of some kind into our test apparatus, it would certainly produce hesitation. We should expect, then, that punishment would also produce greater resistance to extinction in an appropriate situation. What do the data on punishment show?

At first glance, the series of studies done by Maier and his students (Maier, 1949) on fixation of response following punishment in an insoluble discrimination problem seem to confirm our theory. Most of these studies have used a jumping stand with two windows to choose between. The "correct window" is varied randomly so that learning cannot occur. The "incorrect window" is always locked so that, if the animal jumps to it, it bumps its nose and falls down. The result of this procedure is that an appreciable number of animals become "fixated" on one window and do not learn even when the problem becomes solvable. Superficially, and loosely, these results would seem to be compatible with dissonance theory. Perhaps the fixation occurs because of some very strong extra attraction that has developed. On closer investigation, however, any such interpretation proves to be most implausible, bordering on nonsense. One finds that the reaction of the animals to the punishment is really to discontinue the activity. They refuse to jump. In order to make them jump one must give them considerable punishment on the jumping stand itself, thereby forcing them to jump in order to escape punishment. Certainly, it is unclear what dissonance theory would or could predict when such a procedure is used.

One study, by Klee (1944), attempted to dispense with punishment on the jumping stand. Klee fed his rats only when they jumped to the correct window. They were not fed at all in their cages. If a rat refused to jump, Klee left it on the jumping stand for several hours before returning it to its cage. Such an animal then had nothing to eat until the next day, when it again had an opportunity to jump. Presumably, such an experiment should have been decisive. Unfortunately, the number of rats that starved to death rather than jump is extremely large. In other words, this whole series of experiments does not fit our theoretical conditions. The animals do not continue to engage in an activity while having information that would lead them to discontinue it. On the contrary, they refuse to engage in the activity. Most of the experiments on punishment suffer from the same kind of difficulties from our point of view. The animals almost always have to be forced to engage in the activity which is punished.

Logan (1960, p. 220), however, reports an experiment that seems to avoid this difficulty and finds results that are intriguing. He ran three groups of rats in a straight runway to food. One group experienced shock in the runway on each trial, another experienced the shock on 50 per cent of its trials, and the third group never experienced any shock. During acquisition, the "No Shock Group" ran fastest, as might be expected; the "Partial Shock Group" ran next fastest; and the "100 Per Cent Shock Group," by the end of acquisition, showed serious deterioration of performance. This last group, in essence, showed signs of discontinuing the activity.

Extinction trials were run with neither food nor shock. The data on how resistant these animals were to extinction are of interest to us here, particularly for the "No Shock Group" and the "Partial Shock Group," both of which continued to engage in the activity. The "No Shock Group" extinguishes quite rapidly. The "Partial Shock Group," however, continues to run relatively fast. The average speeds for the two groups cross very early in extinction, and the "Partial Shock Group" continues thereafter to run faster than the "No Shock Group." Logan offers no explanation of these results. They are, however, clearly consistent with what one would expect from dissonance theory. Such results are encouraging, but in view of the possible complex effects of shock, it would be desirable to have additional confirmatory evidence.

Another interesting question that arises from our operational definition of dissonance-producing variables concerns the distinction between incentives and deterrents. If we increased the amount of effort involved in our test apparatus, we would observe slower running, and we would conclude that effort is a deterrent to action and that information concerning effort is dissonant with continuing the activity. If, however, we decreased the amount of food an animal obtains, we would also observe slower running. We would not want to conclude that a small amount of food is a deterrent or that the knowledge that food is obtained is dissonant with continuing to engage in the activity, for we know that food is an incentive. Consequently there seems to be a problem with our operational measure. Clearly, however, this is not a difficult operational problem, since one distinction may easily be applied in the situation. If one increases the magnitude of some variable and observes hesitation of behavior, one may conclude that the variable is a deterrent. If one decreases the magnitude of the variable and then observes slower behavior, one may conclude that it is an incentive.

According to the analysis one would make from dissonance theory, this distinction between deterrents and incentives is rather crucial. We should not want to say that any magnitude of incentive, however small, introduces dissonance with con-

tinuing to engage in the activity. There are data in the literature (Armus, 1959), however, showing that after training with
100 per cent reward, rats that obtained a large amount of food
extinguished more quickly than rats that obtained a small
amount. In other words, decreasing the amount of reward has
exactly the same effects in our test apparatus and in extinction
as increasing the delay of reward, effort, or any deterrent. Thus,
from these data it might appear that the distinction between
deterrent and incentive is not an essential one.

However, if we look at the theory and the data closely, the
distinction between incentive and deterrent remains a crucial
distinction. Let us recall the kinds of results that were obtained
with variables that were clearly deterrents. The effort variable
is a good example of this. As effort during acquisition was
increased, resistance to extinction increased. This was true
whether one was dealing with 100 per cent reward situations or
with partial reward situations. This uniformity of effect, however, was not found in connection with an incentive such as
magnitude of reward. It will be remembered from our discussion in Chapter 7 that Hulse (1958) reports that smaller magnitude of reward leads to greater resistance to extinction after 100
per cent reward, but leads to *less* resistance to extinction after
partial reward. Clearly, incentives and deterrents do not produce the same results and must be distinguished operationally
and conceptually. The conceptual distinction between incentives and deterrents which is made in our theory enabled us to
explain this pattern of results.

## What variables affect the magnitude of dissonance and what variables affect how much extra attraction will develop?

The skeletal theoretical statement presented at the beginning of this chapter made no mention of the variables that determine the magnitude of the effects involved. Clearly, for the
theory to be useful, there must be some specification of conditions affecting the magnitude of dissonance and conditions affecting the degree of extra attraction that develops. How have
these variables been specified in the theory, and to what extent
have the data supported the theory in these respects?

It was stated in Chapter 2 that as the magnitude of dissonance increases, the greater will be the attempts to reduce the dissonance and, hence, the greater will be the development of extra attractions in the situation. This statement, however, does not solve any operational problems. We still must identify the variables which affect the magnitude of dissonance. The theoretical exposition in Chapter 2 also states that as the magnitude of a deterrent increases, the magnitude of the dissonance created by continuing to engage in the action also increases. This statement, of course, enables us to look at the data to see what corroboration is offered.

In connection with partial reward, it is by no means immediately obvious what one means by the magnitude of the deterrent. One's first thought might be that the magnitude of the deterrent is to be interpreted as meaning the relative frequency of unrewarded trials. But we have clearly demonstrated that this is not the case. The resistance to extinction seems to be a function only of the number of instances of unrewarded trials, not of their relative frequency (Experiment 5, Chapter 4). Indeed, we were led to do Experiment 5 because it seemed likely that the magnitude of dissonance experienced on any trial would be determined by the things that happened on that specific trial. Further, if this suggestion is correct, it seems plausible to specify that the magnitude of the deterrent depends on how much reward is expected on unrewarded trials. The point in mentioning this again is to show some of the relative vagueness that exists in parts of our theoretical statement. It is not always clear what operations correspond to the theoretical requirements.

On the other hand, the specific operational manipulations that increase the magnitude of dissonance are reasonably clear in connection with other variables. For delay of reward, the theory would imply that the longer the delay, the greater the magnitude of the deterrent, and the stronger should be the effect. Whatever data exist in the literature tend to give some support to this, but the data are scanty. We ourselves have not investigated it at all. We have, however, devoted considerable attention to the variable of effort. Here again, we should expect that the greater the effort expended, the greater would be the dissonance created. In general, our findings have supported this. When greater effort is required during acquisition, regardless of whether the reward is partial or 100 per cent, the organism is more resistant to extinction.

We have said relatively little about the process by means of which the animal develops some extra attractions in a situation in order to reduce dissonance. Nor have we said much about variables which would affect the rapidity and effectiveness with which such dissonance reduction is accomplished. In the human being there are a whole variety of dissonance reduction mechanisms which seem to be effective, but this is probably not true in a non-verbal organism like the rat. We have therefore tried to specify a dissonance reduction mechanism that would seem reasonable in a non-verbal organism. We assumed that, when dissonance exists, the animal is able to discover things in the situation, or in the activity, that satisfy its other subordinate motives. If this suggestion is correct, then a number of interesting questions may be raised.

Presumably, if the animal is able to find things that satisfy subordinate motives, these motives must exist within the animal rather constantly. If the animal is dominated by some strong need such as hunger, these subordinate motives may remain latent and not affect the animal's behavior. When dissonance exists, however, these other motives may become more salient. Still, it would seem plausible to argue that as long as an organism is dominated by some strong drive, it is unlikely that these other motives would affect behavior strongly. Such reasoning leads one to the speculation that, if an animal experienced strong dissonance under conditions of general weak motivation, dissonance reduction might be more effective and more pronounced behavioral consequences would be observed. These considerations led us to do the experiments reported in Chapter 6 using minimal motivation during extinction. These experiments did show that the effects of dissonance reduction were observable under minimal motivation conditions, but we produced little evidence to support the notion that these effects are stronger under low than under high motivation.

It is perplexing that so little work has been done on rats

under conditions of weak motivation. When psychological research is done on humans, it is almost always under conditions of weak motivation, but on animals almost always the opposite. It is interesting to speculate that this may be one of the reasons for the great difficulty of integrating research on animals with research on humans. Behavior may be very different when a single strong drive does not dominate. Harlow, Harlow, and Meyer (1950) report some interesting data related to this. Monkeys show an intrinsic interest in certain kinds of puzzles and will work on them for long periods of time. If, however, they are given the experience of getting food by solving these puzzles, their performance deteriorates. Certainly, more study of behavior under weak motivation is needed.

One other interesting point may be raised on the basis of our hunch about the process of dissonance reduction in the rat: if the rat reduces dissonance by finding elements in the situation that satisfy other existing motives, then the characteristics of the situation in which it finds itself will be an important determinant of how effectively it can reduce dissonance. Psychologists who work with rats are in the habit of using extremely barren situations for their experiments. There are, of course, reasons for this—the more barren the experimental apparatus, the easier it is to control relevant variables. But if our speculations are correct, a very barren experimental situation limits the possibility of the organism to reduce dissonance. Perhaps if the experimental environments were richer, more like the environments to be found in the natural habitat of the organism, the effects one would observe would be stronger. Surely, the natural habitat of an animal must possess many aspects capable of satisfying a wide variety of subordinate motives. We should like to stress, however, that this particular mechanism for reducing dissonance is not the only one available, nor is it probably available to all organisms. Higher organisms undoubtedly have additional techniques for dissonance reduction. Humans certainly have, and we would speculate that the higher the phylogenetic development of the animal, the greater the variety and effectiveness of its dissonance-reducing mechanisms. Certainly, dissonance reduction effects that can be shown only with difficulty in the rat can be shown easily in the human. We would anticipate that in a monkey, for example, intermediate magnitudes of effects would be found. And, as we pointed out in Chapter 2, lower organisms such as fish are probably very ineffective at dissonance reduction. Indeed, in fish, partial reward does not increase resistance to extinction.

*How can we measure the amount of extra attraction that an organism has developed as a result of dissonance reduction?*

In order to test our theoretical statement, we must have some way of measuring, behaviorally, whether or not, and the extent to which, any extra attraction has developed in a situation. We have, of course, dealt with this problem extensively, particularly in Chapter 3. But a fresh look at how we have dealt with this problem indicates that the solutions we have reached are not very adequate. We reached the conclusion that resistance to extinction was the best available indication of the existence of extra attraction. It may be that it is the best available measure in the sense that it is the only one that gives consistent results in the theoretically expected directions, but it must be admitted that it remains very indirect. Presumably, if extra attraction has been developed in a situation, this should act as an incentive for the animal. It seems odd, and certainly a bit indirect, to measure the value of an *incentive* by observing how rapidly an animal *stops* going to the place toward which it is supposed to be attracted.

If one could demonstrate that, in the absence of any extrinsic reward, an animal will learn a new action in order to get somewhere, this would be more direct and more convincing evidence of some intrinsic incentive in the situation. Let us remember at this point, however, that we have data showing our inability to demonstrate a differential in new learning between a group that theoretically had developed extra attractions and a group that had not. In two experiments, both reported in Chapter 6, we compared such groups of animals in a new learning situation. In one experiment (Experiment 12) they had to learn to press a bar in order to get into the box where extra attractions had presumably developed. In the other experiment (Experiment

13) they had to run a four-unit T-maze. In neither experiment were any differences found between the two groups of animals. Peculiarly, it was not that neither group learned the new task. Both of them learned it rather rapidly—a peculiarity we do not understand. The important thing is that we obtained no difference between those that had presumably developed extra attractions and those that had not.

What are the implications of our failure to demonstrate a differential in learning a new task, and how can we explain this failure? It is easy to say something like "the more one changes the total situation from the original one, the less does one observe the effects of the extra attraction." But such a statement does not explain anything. It is also easy to say that the extra attraction is probably rather weak and hence does not show itself when the task is too difficult. But this is more an excuse than an explanation. Even if the extra attraction is weak, why should it not show itself, at least weakly? On the other hand, we do see the effects of these extra attractions in extinction. Here they seem reasonably stable. Indeed, when extinction trials were run under very low motivation conditions, thus reducing competing motives, there was little evidence of any true extinction process (Experiments 9, 10, and 11). One is almost forced to conclude that a new test situation produces stimuli and behavior (perhaps exploratory) that result in a diminution of the strength of the extra attractions. We have, however, devoted little attention to discussing and analyzing the conditions under which extra attraction will decrease. The only thing we have said is that, if there are competing incentives that cause the animal to decide *not* to go to the place in which it has developed extra attractions, this decision will cause a reversal of the process and the extra attraction will begin to break down. This may be pertinent to the new learning task if a wholly new situation evokes such competing motives. Unless there are such refusals, explicit or implicit, to go to the place that possesses extra attractions, we would not expect them to have weakened, since there is no plausible reason to assume that simple disuse would cause the extra attractions to disappear. All of this reasoning is rather *ad hoc*, but unfortunately we have no better solutions to offer.

It would be unfair to end this chapter, and the book, with only a summary of the difficulties and ambiguities that exist in the theory and the data we have presented. Many things are clear, a number of previously unexplained facts are adequately covered by our theory, and, what is more, we have uncovered several new phenomena. Perhaps the best summary we can make of the positive contribution that this volume represents is to list these new findings:

1. Resistance to extinction after partial reward is *not* a function of the ratio of rewarded to unrewarded trials during acquisition. It is a function of the total number of unrewarded trials.
2. If an animal is never rewarded in a given place but only delayed there, it will continue to run to that place during extinction longer than will animals that have either always been rewarded in that place or have been partially rewarded there.
3. If, before extinction trials are run, the animals are taken off their deprivation schedule so that they are no longer hungry, the same or even greater differences in resistance to extinction are obtained than would be the case if the animals were hungry during extinction.
4. Partial reward effects are obtained even though the absence of reward which disconfirms an expectation is *never* associated with the response measured during extinction.
5. Increasing the effort that an animal must expend in order to reach a reward increases the resistance to extinction.

It seems to us that these findings, together with the other results that we have discussed in the book, are very difficult to explain by any of the other existing theories. We saw in Chapter 2 that the attempts at explaining partial reward effects by Sheffield (1949) and Weinstock (1954) could not adequately account for the experimental evidence. We saw, in addition, in Chapter 4, that the expectancy idea, as proposed by Humphreys (1939), or any form of discrimination hypothesis is also inadequate. We saw in Chapter 5 that the frustration hypothesis, as proposed by Amsel (1958), cannot be applied to explain our data concerning the effects of zero reward. Furthermore, as we have pointed out, none of the previously proposed theories has integrated partial reward, delay of reward, and effort expenditure.

Our own explanation, of course, is neither perfect nor fully developed. Nonetheless, it provides a basis for explaining many puzzling experimental results and for integrating a variety of variables. Its strength stems largely from the fact that it inverts the traditional way of looking at such factors as non-reward, delay of reward, and effort, all of which have historically been viewed as inhibitors of behavior. Though not denying this aspect of their influence, we have regarded them as having, in addition, a facilitative effect. They indirectly create attractions or incentives in the situation. They do this by creating dissonance in the animal and thus leading it to discover additional satisfactions. It perhaps needs to be emphasized that these additional satisfactions, or extra attractions, are developed through a process quite different from secondary reward. Indeed, it is almost opposite to secondary reward in that *lack of rewards* leads to their development. On the other hand, both the dissonance reduction process and secondary reward may be seen as means of developing "secondary reinforcers." This term is, of course, purely descriptive, indicating simply that past experience of an unspecified nature has made a previously neutral set of stimuli into potential "reinforcers" of behavior. The use of this term, however, helps us to fit our own contribution into the general context of learning and learning theory. What we have proposed is a new mechanism by means of which "secondary reinforcers" sometimes develop.

The specific process of dissonance reduction does, however, invert many of the customary ways of looking at and explaining learning and extinction. We are aware that this inversion of the usual modes of explanation may not find easy acceptance, but the fact that it leads to the clarification of a considerable number of problems gives us hope for its future.

# References

1. Aiken, E. G. (1957) The effort variable in the acquisition, extinction, and spontaneous recovery of an instrumental response. *J. exp. Psychol.*, 53 : 47–51.
2. Amsel, A. (1958) The role of frustrative nonreward in noncontinuous reward situations. *Psychol. Bull.*, 55 : 102–19.
3. Anderson, E. E. (1941) The externalization of drive. III. Maze learning by non-rewarded and by satiated rats. *J. genet. Psychol.*, 59 : 397–426.
4. Applezweig, M. H. (1951) Response potential as a function of effort. *J. comp., physiol. Psychol.*, 44 : 225–35.
5. Armus, H. L. (1959) Effect of magnitude of reinforcement on acquisition and extinction of a running response. *J. exp. Psychol.*, 58 : 61–63.
6. Aronson, E. (1961) The effect of effort on the attractiveness of rewarded and unrewarded stimuli. *J. abnorm. soc. Psychol.*, in press.
7. Aronson, E., and Mills, J. (1959) The effect of severity of initiation on liking for a group. *J. abnorm. soc. Psychol.*, 59 : 177–81.
8. Bitterman, M. E., Feddersen, W. E., and Tyler, D. W. (1953) Secondary reinforcement and the discrimination hypothesis. *Amer. J. Psychol.*, 66 : 456–64.
9. Brunswik, E. (1939) Probability as a determiner of rat behavior. *J. exp. Psychol.*, 25 : 175–97.
10. Capaldi, E. J. (1958) The effect of different amounts of training on the resistance to extinction of different patterns of partially reinforced responses. *J. comp. physiol. Psychol.*, 51 : 367–71.
11. D'Amato, M. R., Lachman, R., and Kivy, P. (1958) Secondary reinforcement as affected by reward schedule and the testing situation. *J. comp. physiol. Psychol.*, 51 : 737–41.
12. Elam, C. B., Tyler, D. W., and Bitterman, M. E. (1954) A fur-

ther study of secondary reinforcement and the discrimination hypothesis. *J. comp. physiol. Psychol.,* 47 : 381–84.

13. Estes, W. K. (1959) The statistical approach to learning theory. In Koch, S. (ed.) *Psychology: A study of a science.* Vol. 2. New York: McGraw-Hill.

14. Fehrer, E. (1956) Effects of amount of reinforcement and of pre- and post reinforcement delays on learning and extinction. *J. exp. Psychol.,* 52 : 167–76.

15. Festinger, L. (1957) *A theory of cognitive dissonance.* Stanford, Calif.: Stanford University Press.

16. Goodrich, K. P. (1959) Performance in different segments of an instrumental response chain as a function of reinforcement schedule. *J. exp. Psychol.,* 57 : 57–63.

17. Grosslight, J. H., and Radlow, R. (1956) Patterning effect of the nonreinforcement-reinforcement sequence in a discrimination situation. *J. comp. physiol. Psychol.,* 49 : 542–46.

18. Grosslight, J. H., and Radlow, R. (1957) Patterning effect of the nonreinforcement-reinforcement sequence involving a single nonreinforced trial. *J. comp. physiol. Psychol.,* 50 : 23–25.

19. Harlow, H. F., Harlow, M. K., and Meyer, D. R. (1950) Learning motivated by a manipulation drive. *J. exp. Psychol.,* 40 : 228–34.

20. Hull, C. L. (1943) *Principles of behavior.* New York: Appleton-Century.

21. Hulse, S. H., Jr. (1958) Amount and percentage of reinforcement and duration of goal confinement in conditioning and extinction. *J. exp. Psychol.,* 56 : 48–57.

22. Hulse, S. H., Jr., and Stanley, W. C. (1956) Extinction by omission of food as related to partial and secondary reinforcement. *J. exp. Psychol.,* 52 : 221–27.

23. Humphreys, L. G. (1939) The effect of random alternation of reinforcement on the acquisition and extinction of conditioned eyelid reactions. *J. exp. Psychol.,* 25 : 141–58.

24. Jenkins, W. O., and Stanley, J. C., Jr. (1950) Partial reinforcement: A review and critique. *Psychol. Bull.,* 47 : 193–234.

25. Katz, S. (1957) Stimulus aftereffects and the partial-reinforcement extinction effect. *J. exp. Psychol.,* 53 : 167–72.

26. Kimble, G. A. (1961) *Conditioning and learning.* New York: Appleton-Century-Crofts.

27. Klee, J. B. (1944) The relation of frustration and motivation to the production of abnormal fixations in the rat. *Psychol. Monographs,* 56 : No. 257.

28. Klein, R. M. (1959) Intermittent primary reinforcement as a parameter of secondary reinforcement. *J. exp. Psychol.,* 58 : 423–27.

29. Lewis, D. J. (1956) Acquisition, extinction, and spontaneous recovery as a function of percentage of reinforcement and intertrial interval. *J. exp. Psychol.*, 51: 45–53.

30. ———. (1960) Partial reinforcement: A selective review of the literature since 1950. *Psychol. Bull.*, 57: 1–28.

31. Lewis, D. J., and Cotton, J. W. (1958) Partial reinforcement and non-response acquisition. *J. comp. physiol. Psychol.*, 51: 251–54.

32. Lewis, D. J., and Cotton, J. W. (1959) The effect of intertrial interval and number of acquisition trials with partial reinforcement on performance. *J. comp. physiol. Psychol.*, 52: 598–601.

33. Logan, F. A. (1952) The role of delay of reinforcement in determining reaction potential. *J. exp. Psychol.*, 43: 393–99.

34. ———. (1960) *Incentive.* New Haven: Yale University Press.

35. Longo, N., and Bitterman, M. E. (1960) The effect of partial reinforcement with spaced practice on resistance to extinction in the fish. *J. comp. physiol. Psychol.*, 53: 169–72.

36. Maatsch, J. L., Adelman, H. M., and Denny, M. R. (1954) Effort and resistance to extinction of the bar-pressing response. *J. comp. physiol. Psychol.*, 47: 47–50.

37. Maier, N. R. F. (1949) *Frustration, a study of behavior without a goal.* New York: McGraw-Hill.

38. Marx, M. H. (1960) Resistance to extinction as a function of degree of reproduction of training conditions. *J. exp. Psychol.*, 59: 337–42.

39. Mason, D. J. (1957) The relation of secondary reinforcement to partial reinforcement. *J. comp. physiol. Psychol.*, 50: 264–68.

40. Mowrer, O. H. (1960) *Learning theory and behavior.* New York: Wiley.

41. Myers, A. K., and Miller, N. E. (1954) Failure to find a learned drive based on hunger; evidence for learning motivated by "exploration." *J. comp. physiol. Psychol.*, 47: 428–36.

42. Myers, J. L. (1958) Secondary reinforcement: A review of recent experimentation. *Psychol. Bull.*, 55: 284–301.

43. Saltzman, I. J. (1949) Maze learning in the absence of primary reinforcement: A study of secondary reinforcement. *J. comp. physiol. Psychol.*, 42: 161–73.

44. Seward, J. P., and Procter, D. M. (1960) Performance as a function of drive, reward, and habit-strength. *Amer. J. Psychol.*, 73: 448–53.

45. Sheffield, V. F. (1949) Extinction as a function of partial reinforcement and distribution of practice. *J. exp. Psychol.*, 39: 511–26.

46. Spence, K. W. (1960) *Behavior theory and learning.* Englewood Cliffs, N.J.: Prentice-Hall.

47. Theios, J. (1961) The partial reinforcement effect sustained through blocks of continuous reinforcement. Ph.D. Dissertation, Stanford University. (In press. *J. exp. Psychol.*, 1962.)

48. Thompson, M. E. (1944) An experimental investigation of the gradient of reinforcement in maze learning. *J. exp. Psychol.*, 34: 390–403.

49. Tyler, D. W., Wortz, E. C., and Bitterman, M. E. (1953) The effect of random and alternating partial reinforcement on resistance to extinction in the rat. *Amer. J. Psychol.*, 66: 57–65.

50. Wagner, A. R. (1959) The role of reinforcement and non reinforcement in an "apparent frustration effect." *J. exp. Psychol.*, 57: 130–36.

51. Weinstock, M. G. (1957) A factorial study of some variables affecting resistance to extinction under partial reinforcement with spaced trials. Ph.D. Dissertation, Indiana University.

52. Weinstock, S. (1954) Resistance to extinction of a running response following partial reinforcement under widely spaced trials. *J. comp. physiol. Psychol.*, 47: 318–23.

53. Weiss, R. F. (1961) Response speed, amplitude, and resistance to extinction as joint functions of work and length of behavior chain. *J. exp. Psychol.*, 61: 245–56.

54. Wike, E. L., Kintsch, W., and Gutekunst, R. (1959) Patterning effects in partially delayed reinforcement. *J. comp. physiol. Psychol.*, 52: 411–14.

55. Wike, E. L., and McNamara, H. J. (1957) The effects of percentage of partially delayed reinforcement on the acquisition and extinction of an instrumental response. *J. comp. physiol. Psychol.*, 50: 348–51.

56. Wilson, W., Weiss, E. J., and Amsel, A. (1955) Two tests of the Sheffield hypothesis concerning resistance to extinction, partial reinforcement, and distribution of practice. *J. exp. Psychol.*, 50: 51–60.

57. Wodinsky, J., and Bitterman, M. E. (1959) Partial reinforcement in the fish. *J. Amer. Psychol.*, 72: 184–99.

58. Wodinsky, J., and Bitterman, M. E. (1960) Resistance to extinction in the fish after extensive training with partial reinforcement. *Amer. J. Psychol.*, 73: 429–34.

59. Zimmerman, D. W. (1957) Durable secondary reinforcement: Method and theory. *Psychol. Review*, 64: 373–83.

60. ———. (1959) Sustained performance in rats based on secondary reinforcement. *J. comp. physiol. Psychol.*, 52: 353–58.

# Index

# Index